Change Forces: The Sequel

Educational Change and Development Series

Series Editors: Andy Hargreaves, Ontario Institute for Studies in Education, Canada and
Ivor F Goodson, Warner Graduate School, University of Rochester, USA and Centre for Applied Research in Education, University of East Anglia, Norwich, UK

Change Forces:
The Sequel

Michael Fullan

UK   Falmer Press, 1 Gunpowder Square, London, EC4A 3DE
USA   Falmer Press, Taylor & Francis Inc., 325 Chestnut Street, 8th Floor, Philadelphia, PA 19106

First published in 1999

Reprinted 2000

A catalogue record for this book is available from the British Library

ISBN 0 7507 0756 9 cased
ISBN 0 7507 0755 0 paper

Library of Congress Cataloging-in-Publication Data are available on request

Jacket design by Caroline Archer

Typeset in 11/13pt Garamond by
Graphicraft Limited, Hong Kong

Printed in the United States by George H. Buchanan, Philadelphia, PA.

Contents

Y-39-02 ABC ALG.57

List of Figures

For Vince and Mary

Preface

The original *Change Forces* hit a responsive chord (Fullan, 1993). Using a combination of new theories (in particular, chaos theory) and insights from our own and others' change projects around the world, I identified novel insights and better ways of comprehending overloaded and fragmented educational reform. I criticized and called into question key concepts such as vision and strategic planning, site-based management, strong leadership, collegiality and consensus, accountability and assessment. Not that these ideas were all wrong; rather they contributed to superficial thinking.

It is time now to move even deeper into the analysis and action implications of studying the dynamics of change forces in educational reform. The field is richer in theory and more sophisticated in empirical investigation than it was five years ago. *Change Forces: The Sequel* focuses on the exciting progress that has been made very recently in thinking about and strategizing about organizational and policy reform. As before, myths are debunked and new insights are advanced. We will see that the concept of moral purpose — improvements designed to make a difference in the lives of students — is not as straightforward as it seems. We will unlock the black box of why collaborative cultures really work, and what it takes to sustain them. We will see that breakthroughs occur when we begin to think of conflict, diversity and resistance as positive, absolutely essential forces for success. We will probe deeply into the role of knowledge inside learning organizations, as well as knowledge and outside connections. We will learn from chaos and complexity theory, and evolutionary theory that learning occurs on the edge of chaos, where a delicate balance must be maintained between too much and too little structure. We will understand that 'anxiety containing' strategies are essential under such circumstances. We will appreciate how 'inside-out' and 'outside-in' orientations to change at the school level must come together. We will also unpack the problem of transferability — why obvious good ideas do not get used by others, and how to reframe the matter so that larger-scale change becomes possible. Finally, we will come to appreciate the essential fusion of intellectual, political and spiritual forces.

As before, I draw heavily on new business books on organizational learning. Although that literature as a whole suffers from superficiality, there are some absolute gems of studies that have profound implications for change in school systems. I have learned also from several large-scale change evaluation studies. Over the past few years, we have been engaged in the study of the Holmes Group for the Ford Foundation, the evaluation of the Building Infrastructure for Professional Development project for Rockefeller, the assessment of the Learning Labs initiative for the National Education Association and the Manitoba School Improvement Program for the Gordon Foundation. All of these studies and others have been great wellsprings of knowledge about change forces. I thank, in particular, Nancy Watson who has been my co-investigator in most of these endeavors.

As to the scope of applicability of the book, I do draw on North American literature and cases for most of the specific examples and illustrations. Our work in different parts of the world does, however, provide evidence of a much more comprehensive relevance. The core concepts are applicable across the world, whether we consider Eastern Europe, Asia, Australia, New Zealand, the United Kingdom and other places where dynamic change has been studied. My apologies for not doing justice to this international research, but my familiarity with North America is more conducive to using clear examples of complex concepts from this source. Be that as it may, I do use references from work in other parts of the world. The lessons of change forces are indeed a worldwide phenomenon.

Writing is always a source of development of new ideas as well as dissemination. One series has been particularly stimulating, namely the *What's Worth Fighting For* trilogy with my colleague Andy Hargreaves, which we did for the Elementary Teachers' Federation of Ontario (Fullan, 1997; Fullan and Hargreaves, 1992; Hargreaves and Fullan, 1998), and the corresponding video, which captures this work in several cities in North America — Toronto, Winnipeg, Chicago and New Orleans (Video Journal of Education, 1998).

Understanding change is just as much a matter of 'doing' reform as it is studying it. I have been fortunate to be part of several 'living laboratories' of change. The longstanding Learning Consortium in Ontario, the more recent Peel University Partnership, and the Manitoba School Improvement Program have been three vital examples of partnerships within which we have both accomplished significant improvements while learning more about the complexities and dynamics of change.

Perhaps even more telling is the transformation of higher education in which I have been engaged as Dean in two evolving situations over the past decade. First, at the Faculty of Education, University of Toronto we tried to practice what we preach about change as we immersed ourselves in the renewal of that faculty over the 1988–96 period (Fullan, 1998). More recently, the merger of the latter faculty with the Ontario Institute for Studies in Education has provided us with the ultimate living laboratory of complex reform. The new institution, called OISE/UT, started in July 1996 and represents the combined merger of almost 200 education faculty, more than 150 administrative staff, 9,000 students ranging across pre-service, in-service and graduate programs, two lab schools and several field centers across the Province of Ontario. Developing a new culture from two previous cultures, decertification of unions involving overlapping membership, massive reorganization and new leadership have given all of us daily firsthand experience with the forces of change. I have learned a great deal about change from my colleagues in this large-scale renewal as we are engaged in developing the capacities of a complex higher education organization to play a significant partnership role in improving educational systems.

I have been blessed, then, with multifaceted occasions to revel in dynamic change situations. My colleagues at home and abroad are too numerous to mention, but I thank them all for the privilege of learning with them. The one exception who I will name is the late Matt Miles. For years Matt was my full-time mentor and part-time tormentor (as he demanded ever more clarity of thinking). The field suffers from the loss of this superb student of change, and I miss him greatly.

My thanks also to Joan Domonchuk who prepared the manuscript under very tight timelines, and to Andy Hargreaves and Blair Mascall for their comments.

As I look ahead, I am excited to say that *Change Forces* will also become a trilogy. The current publication, *Change Forces: The Sequel* will be followed in 2001 with the third entry, *Change Forces with a Vengeance* (an appropriate title for the new millennium). We are at such an early stage of new developments that the next few years should continue to yield rich new insights.

Finally, my change team at home continues to thrive, always supportive and lovingly demanding. Thank you Wendy, Bailey and Conor — may the forces of change continue to be with you.

Chapter 1

Moral Purpose and Complexity

*The ability to assume complexity is a great strength. You could call
it the ability to deal with reality.*

(Saul, 1997, p. 222)

Once upon a time the moral purpose of educational reform seemed
relatively straightforward. While we knew that innovation was often
motivated by politics and careerism, most people when pushed would
agree that the ultimate purpose of reform is to benefit all students. If the
problem were that straightforward, that simple, we would have solved
it long ago. After all, we have been innovating for student improvement for most of this century. The direct approach of naming the goal
and mobilizing to achieve it does not, and cannot, work in something
as complex as moral change agentry — a continuous preoccupation
with making virtuous improvements in a world in which the particular pathways to success are literally unknowable in advance of doing
something.

At the micro level, moral purpose in education means making a
difference in the life-chances of all students — more of a difference for
the disadvantaged because they have further to go. At the macro level,
moral purpose is education's contribution to societal development and
democracy. A strong public school system, as I shall argue, is the key to
social, political and economic renewal in society. In postmodern society, more than ever before, a strong commitment to the role of moral
purpose in educational reform is crucial. But because of worldwide
diversity, and because of chaotic complexity, figuring out moral purpose,
getting or staying committed to it and making progress in achieving it
are enormously difficult. At the very time we need more of a moral
commitment to the public good, the forces of change are creating
confusion, frustration and discouragement. This book is about pursuing
moral purpose in complex times.

There are two primary reasons why achieving moral purpose is
complex. One concerns the dynamics of diversity, equity and power; the
other involves the concept and reality of complexity itself.

Diversity, Equity and Power

Diversity means different races, different interest groups, different power bases and basically different lots in life. To achieve moral purpose is to forge interaction and even mutual interest across groups. Yet the problem is that there are great tendencies to keep people different than ourselves at a distance. In psychological experiments people are more likely to exhibit helpful behavior to those similar to themselves. As Sober and Wilson (1998, pp. 326–7) observe:

> If empathy elicits altruistic motives with respect to those whom we take to be similar, its absence means that we are less inclined to be altruistically motivated toward those whom we take to be different.

You cannot achieve moral purpose unless you develop mutual empathy and relationships across diverse groups, and this is no easy task. As we will see later, there are ways of conceptualizing, valuing and working through the discomfort of each other's diversity, but these require very different strategies than we are accustomed to. Having empathy for those who are different from ourselves is a tall but essential order.

We also have to recognize that many reforms — equity-minded reforms in particular — are not in the short-term interests (more about long-term interests later) of those in privileged positions. Oakes *et al.* (1998, p. 953) provide theoretical and empirical evidence to back up their claim: 'We find that when reforms seek to achieve parity in opportunity and achievement across diverse groups of students, reformers faced enormous challenges.' They argue that the change literature falls short because it takes a neutral stance towards equity and power. In their study of detracking in ten racially and socio-economically mixed secondary schools, Oakes *et al.* found that teacher and principal change agents got blindsided by fellow teachers and powerful parents opposing detracking (moving from homogeneous to mixed-ability classes). The change leaders in these cases failed to realize (and the change literature provided little help) that intense opposition to detracking was based on perceived loss of advantage to higher income, white students if they were mixed with lower income, predominantly non-white students.

Similarly, Slee, Weiner and Tomlinson (1998) and others launch a fundamental critique of school effectiveness and school improvement, not so much for what these movements study, but rather what they leave out or underemphasize. They argue that social class is relegated to a control variable and not treated as problematic in its own right, that there is a failure to focus on power, and that school effectiveness research tends to concentrate on management issues and broad generalizations rather than on the complexity of the issues faced by teachers operating in disadvantaged circumstances.

Slee, Weiner *et al.* themselves are short on solutions, but along with Oakes and her colleagues they are essentially right in calling for a more critical preoccupation on the part of researchers, policymakers and teachers with issues of power and equity in the improvement process.

These problems, based as they are on power and privilege, may seem insurmountable. And critical theorists, as correct in their analysis as they may be, have offered little by way of strategy beyond brute sanity (to be sure, this is an enormously difficult issue to address strategically). There may, however, be other resources and ideas available for accomplishing more comprehensive and equitable reform, which brings us to complexity theory and evolutionary theory.

Complexity and Evolution

The paradox of complexity is that it makes things exceedingly difficult, while the answer lies within its natural dynamics — dynamics which can be designed and stimulated in the right direction, but can never be controlled.

The jury surely must be in by now that rationally constructed reform strategies do not work. The reason is that such strategies can never work in the face of rapidly changing environments. Further, rapid change is endemic and inevitable in postmodern society — a system which self-generates complex dynamics over and over and over again. As Stacey (1996a) puts it:

> Most textbooks focus heavily on techniques and procedures for long-term planning, on the need for visions and missions, on the importance and the means of securing strongly shared cultures, on the equation of success with consensus, consistency, uniformity and order. [However, in complex environments] the real management task is that of coping with and even using unpredictability, clashing counter-cultures, disensus, contention, conflict, and inconsistency. In short, the task that justifies the existence of all managers has to do with instability, irregularity, difference and disorder. (pp. xix–xx)

The old way of managing change, appropriate in more stable times, does not work anymore. Two theories in particular help us think differently about where we are at the end of the twentieth century, and how we must approach the new millennium, — complexity theory and evolutionary theory.

Complexity Theory

Complexity and chaos theory are the same thing, but I prefer the former label because it is more accurately descriptive. This new science of complexity essentially claims that the link between cause and effect is difficult to trace, that change (planned and otherwise) unfolds in non-linear ways, that paradoxes and contradictions abound and that creative solutions arise out of interaction under conditions of uncertainty, diversity and instability.

Stacey (1996a) captures the essence of complexity theory in these words:

> A complexity theory of organization is built on the following propositions:
> - All organizations are webs of nonlinear feedback loops connected to other people and organizations (its environments) by webs of nonlinear feedback loops.
> - Such nonlinear feedback systems are capable of operating in states of stable and unstable equilibrium, or in the borders between these states, that is far-from-equilibrium, in bounded instability at the edge of chaos.
> - All organizations are paradoxes. They are powerfully pulled towards stability by the forces of integration, maintenance controls, human desires for security and certainty, and adaptation to the environment on the one hand. They are also powerfully pulled to the opposite extreme of unstable equilibrium by the forces of division and decentralization, human desires for excitement and innovation, and isolation from the environment.
> - If the organization gives in to the pull to stability it fails because it becomes ossified and cannot change easily. If it gives in to the pull to instability it disintegrates. Success lies in sustaining an organization in the borders between stability and instability. This is a state of chaos, a difficult-to-maintain dissipative structure.
> - The dynamics of the successful organization are therefore those of irregular cycles and discontinuous trends, falling within qualitative patterns, fuzzy but recognizable categories taking the form of archetypes and templates.
> - Because of its own internal dynamic, a successful organization faces completely unknowable specific futures.

- Agents within the system cannot be in control of its long-term future, nor can they install specific frameworks to make it successful, nor can they apply step-by-step analytical reasoning or planning or ideological controls to long-term development. Agents within the system can only do these things in relation to the short term.
- Long-term development is a spontaneously self-organizing process from which new strategic directions may emerge. Spontaneous self-organization is political interaction and learning in groups. Managers have to use reasoning by analogy.
- In this way managers create and discover their environments and the long-term futures of the organizations. (p. 349)

In another book, Stacey (1996b) elaborates on complex adaptive systems:

The science of complexity studies the fundamental properties of nonlinear-feedback networks and particularly of complex adaptive networks. Complex adaptive systems consist of a number of components, or agents, that interact with each other according to sets of rules that require them to examine and respond to each other's behavior in order to improve their behavior and thus the behavior of the system they comprise. In other words, such systems operate in a manner that constitutes learning. Because those learning systems operate in environments that consist mainly of other learning systems, it follows that together they form a co-evolving suprasystem that in a sense creates and learns its way into the future. (p. 10)

Pretty theoretical you say! And yes, this is rocket science, but I will show in subsequent chapters how this theory operates empirically, and how we can use it to more clearly and deeply understand and cope with change.

Brown and Eisenhardt (1998) in their study of twelve global businesses employed complexity theory to help sort out successful from unsuccessful cases. As they put it:

Complexity theory began with an interest in how order springs from chaos. According to complexity theory, adaptation is most effective in systems that are only partially connected. The argument is that too much structure creates gridlock, while too little structure creates chaos. A good example would be the traffic lights in a city. If there are no lights, traffic is chaotic. If there are too many lights, traffic stops. A moderate number of lights creates structure, but still allows drivers to adapt their routes in surprising ways in response to changing traffic conditions. Consequently, the key to effective change is to stay poised on this edge of chaos. Complexity theory focuses managerial thinking on the interrelationships among different parts of an organization and on the trade-off of less control for greater adaptation. (p. 14)

Evolutionary Theory

While complexity theory is about learning and adapting under unstable and uncertain conditions, evolutionary theory of relationships raises the questions of how humans evolve over time, especially in relation to interaction and cooperative behavior. Both Ridley (1996) and Sober and Wilson (1998) trace the evolution of self-centered and cooperative behavior in animals and insects, and in humans. What makes humans different, says Ridley, is culture. Ideas, knowledge, practices, beliefs and the like enter consciousness and can be passed on 'by direct infection from one person to another' (Ridley, 1996, p. 179). And:

> The roots of social order are in our heads, where we possess the instinctive capacities for creating not a perfectly harmonious and virtuous society, but a better one than we have at present. (p. 264)

Ridley raises the interesting evolutionary hypothesis that 'cooperative groups thrive and selfish ones do not, so cooperative societies have survived at the expense of others' (p. 175).

A good example of advantage, if not survival, comes from the story of the titmouse and the robin as reported in Brown and Eisenhardt (1998):

> Coadaptation is most effective when poised between too much and too little structure. The comparison of the structure of social interaction between the titmouse and red robin illustrates this central idea of coadaptation.
>
> In the early 1900s, milk was delivered to homes in the United Kingdom in bottles without caps. Two bird species, the titmouse and the red robin, learned to drink the cream that floated to the tops of the bottles. Eventually, dairy distributors began putting aluminum seals on the bottles to solve this problem. In about twenty years, the population of titmice (about 1 million birds) learned how to pierce the seals. In contrast, the red robins did not. Occasionally, one robin would discover how to pierce the seal, but that knowledge never spread. What is the explanation?
>
> Titmice are social. They travel in flocks of about eight to ten birds for two or three months per year. They communicate some of the time, but not always, and their flocks vary in membership. In contrast,

the red robins are territorial. A male robin will exclude others from his territory. They rarely communicate, and when they do, it is usually antagonistic.

Generally, related agents adapt most effectively when they partially interact with one another. If related agents are always together, then they adapt quickly. However, they have too little diversity to cope with sudden change. If they are never together, the population of agents adapts very slowly to change and may ultimately evolve into a different species that cannot communicate. (p. 75)

De Gues (1997) also takes up the titmouse story as he traces it to the zoologist/biochemist Allan Wilson. In De Gues's (1997) words:

The titmouse went through an extraordinarily successful institutional learning process. The red robins failed, even though individual robins had been as innovative as individual titmice. Moreover, the difference could not be attributed to their ability to communicate. As songbirds, both the titmice and the red robins had the same wide range of means of communication: color, behavior, movements, and song. The explanation, said Professor Wilson, could be found only in the *social propagation* process: the way titmice spread their skill from one individual to members of the species as a whole.

In spring, the titmice live in couples until they have reared their young. By early summer, when the young titmice are flying and feeding on their own, we see the birds moving from garden to garden in flocks of eight to ten individuals. These flocks seem to remain intact, moving together around the countryside, and the period of *mobility* lasts for two to three months.

Red robins, by contrast, are territorial birds. A male robin will not allow another male to enter its territory. When threatened, the robin sends a warning, as if to say, 'Keep the hell out of here.' In general, red robins tend to communicate with each other in an antagonistic manner, with fixed boundaries that they do not cross.

Birds that flock, said Allan Wilson, seem to learn faster. They increase their chances to survive and evolve more quickly. (pp. 134–5, italics in original)

Of course there are countless examples of selfish behavior among individuals and groups. The evolutionary question is whether cooperative relationships serve a higher moral value while at the same time provide individuals or groups with advantages. Culture allows us to recognize, value and build in such advantages over time. We will see in detail later why isolated cultures are less effective than collaborative cultures. We will see that people need each other's knowledge to solve problems. The motivation to share and the opportunity to access information requires ongoing interaction. Interaction is also required for the development and internalization of higher order purposes (moral purposes if you like). Doing and receiving good (or reciprocity) 'only works if people recognize each other' (Ridley, 1996, p. 70). We must, concludes Ridley, 'encourage social and material exchange between equals for that is the raw material of trust, and trust is the foundation of virtue' (p. 265).

But, alas, we don't have enough 'equals' in society for virtue to flourish. Wilkinson (1996) provides a compelling analysis of the 'afflictions of inequality' in his book *Unhealthy Societies*. He reports data as others have found, that it is not the richest societies that have best health, but those that have the smallest income differences between the rich and the poor. In a section on 'How Society Kills', Wilkinson presents a massive amount of worldwide evidence that poor people's lives are terribly affected on a daily basis, and they die at an earlier age on the average. But not just for the obvious reasons of absence of food and exposure to danger. Rather, it is the 'psychosocial pathways' that do the harm. In his words:

> To feel depressed, cheated, bitter, desperate, vulnerable, frightened, angry, worried about debts or job and housing insecurity; to feel devalued, useless, helpless, uncared for, hopeless, isolated, anxious and a failure; these feelings can dominate people's whole experience of life, coloring their experience of everything else. It is the chronic stress arising from feelings like these, which does the damage. It is the social feelings which matter, not exposure to a supposedly toxic material environment. The material environment is merely the indelible mark and constant reminder of the oppressive fact of one's failure, of the atrophy of any sense of having a place in a community, and of one's social exclusion and devaluation as a human being. (Wilkinson, 1996, p. 215)

In other words, prolonged stress damages health.

On the positive side, in situations of greater equality *social cohesion* is the psychosocial pathway to reducing stress and a better life, and the additional good news is that it also means greater economic growth. Lack of supportive relationships is associated with poorer health (not just the absence of friends and close relatives), but also 'less involvement with wider social networks, community activities, etc.' (p. 182). Moreover, Wilkinson (p. 223) presents evidence that greater equity produces greater economic growth (not the other way around).

So the question becomes how to achieve narrower economic income distribution and better social cohesion. Why would those who are better off be concerned with the welfare of others? How do we get people to 'see other members of the public as fellow citizens with whom their welfare is interdependent [rather than seeing] each other as obstacles in each other's way?' (Wilkinson, 1996, p. 155). No one has the answer to this, but it is likely that a combination of political, moral and self-interested forces will be needed.

The first of these three forces concerns political will — the power politics of recognizing that social cohesion, better health and economic productivity are closely associated. As Wilkinson points out, most of the needed policies do not involve direct income transfers from rich to poor, but rather need to be aimed at overcoming the obstacles and disadvantages to people's economic achievement. It is capacity-building that counts, such as investment in early childhood development. Clearly, the moral purpose of educational reform must include capacity-building as a route to individual and societal development.

Second, in evolutionary terms some appeal to the common good and the welfare of others is essential. There is a greater commitment to the common good than there was a century ago (but maybe not greater than five years ago). Moreover, moral purpose and social cohesion can be made more explicit and can be fostered. Wilkinson (1996) points to an experiment that 'illustrates the power of social or moral motivation.' People were interviewed a month prior to filling out their tax returns. In one group, the strict penalties for income tax evasion were stressed; for a second, the moral reasons for tax compliance were emphasized. The finding: 'the moral appeal led to a significantly greater increase in the amount of tax paid' (p. 169). More focus and discussion of moral purpose and more instances of fostering relationships are needed to enhance social cohesion.

Third, and again in evolutionary terms, we may all be better off if greater equity prevails. The results of inequality do not just affect the poor. It costs society more economically to pick up the pieces arising from poverty, and it is more difficult for all of us, including the rich, to live in amoral conflict-ridden societies. More than this, as Wilkinson and others argue, greater equality results in more social cohesion ('at all stages in human society, whether rich or poor, the quality of social relations has been a prime determinant of human welfare and the quality of life', Wilkinson, 1996, p. 211), and in turn greater economic growth. Thus, for example, well-implemented equity-based reforms (such as achieving literacy standards for all children) may be in all of our interests as they result in economic growth in the society as a whole.

We have no reason to be optimistic that these three forces will converge, but at least we now know that moral purpose cannot be approached naively through mission statements and strategic plans.

Moral Purpose and Complexity Together

The overarching argument is best captured in Goerner's (1998) three lessons of 'dynamic evolution':

- *Learning* — Surviving by changing one's mind is a lot more efficient than surviving by changing one's body (that is, waiting for a genetic mutation). We are the wonder of the world today because of this. Yet we cannot rest on our laurels. Learning is never done. It regularly requires that we reorganize what we 'know.'
- *Collaboration* — Learning is done best in groups. The greatest evolutionary leaps have come from independent life forms which learned to work together. Commitment to the greater good is crucial.
- *Intricacy* — Underneath, the rules of dynamic evolution are still at work. Size, for instance, pulls us apart. Failure to stay connected and flowing creates a world designed to crumble. Thus, growth creates regular crisis points which will require we learn anew. The challenge of intricacy is to keep smallness under an ever-growing umbrella of connective tissue. (ch. 7, p. 4)

In educational terms, moral purpose and complexity play themselves out in the relationship between public schools and democracy. In many ways this represents the unfinished legacy of John Dewey. Cohen (1998) argues that Dewey was not child-centered as an end in itself, but rather for the purpose of developing a new system of curriculum and instruction rooted in scientific and social problem-solving through the development of new more democratic social relations. Schools were to become counter-cultural agencies that would 'correct the human and social devastation of industrial capitalism' (Cohen, 1998, p. 427). Need I say that the problem of potential human destruction (and growth) has become compounded in the chaotic conditions of post-modern society.

As Cohen says, Dewey never addressed the problem of how such a public school system could develop let alone thrive in a society that it was to help make over. And we do know that as it has turned out so far, schools are much more a conservative agency for the status quo than a revolutionary force for transformation. But this is indeed the point of this book. Does the public school system have a place in complexity and evolutionary theory as one of the forces pushing toward a higher form of societal development? I believe that it does have an essential role in this transformation, but one that it is not yet nearly capable of performing. 'Change Forces' is about figuring out how to develop the capacity of school systems to become better moral change agents in society.

For starters, developing this capacity means understanding the relationship between democracy and the public school system. In Galbraith's (1996, p. 17) *Good Society*:

> Education not only makes democracy possible; it also makes it essential. Education not only brings into existence a population with an understanding of the public tasks; it also creates their demand to be heard.

Similarly, Saul (1995) says that a primary purpose of education is 'to show individuals how they can function *together* in a society' (p. 138, his italics).

In modern societies the relationship between democracy and schooling has always been too abstract, or perhaps taken for granted and thereby often neglected. It should no longer be. As we said in *What's Worth Fighting For Out There?*: 'Teachers and parents observe democracy deteriorating every time the gap between the privileged and the underprivileged learner widens' (Hargreaves and Fullan, 1998, p. 15). Public schools need to develop what Coleman (1990) termed 'social capital' — to help produce citizens who have the commitment, skills and dispositions to foster norms of civility, compassion, fairness, trust, collaborative engagement and constructive critiques under conditions of great social diversity. Schools also need to develop intellectual capital — problem-solving skills in a technological world — so that all students can learn. This too is a moral purpose. To become committed to the development of social and intellectual capital is to understand the goal of moral purpose; to address it productively is to delve into the intricacies of complexity and change. Moral purpose and complexity need each other.

In summary, moral purpose — making a positive difference in the lives of all citizens — is worth striving for as a value in itself, and because it may eventually be a higher form of evolutionary benefit to humankind. The pathway to moral purpose is a perpetual pursuit because pluralistic (self-centered along with unselfish) motives abound. Narrow self interest and commitment to the common good co-exist. Complexity and evolutionary theory provide powerful guidelines for further development. Intensive human interaction involving people different than ourselves (diversity) provides us with an evolutionary advantage because, (a) interaction is essential to solving problems, and (b) diversity of interaction is most suited to discovering moral and effective solutions to problems presented by turbulent environments. The public school is a critical agency in developing the capacity of individuals and communities to pursue higher moral purpose under conditions of great complexity.

It is no accident that complexity and evolutionary theories are now coming to the fore. The change forces analyzed in this book have become intensified during the 1990s. As we enter the third millennium we are becoming overwhelmed with chaos and disillusionment. But new, more complex ways of thinking, represented by these theories, provide profound, liberating and inspiring possibilities for individuals at all levels of the system to understand better and to act much more effectively.

We are, it must be understood, at the very early stages of human evolutionary development, albeit at a stage that seems to represent a paradigmatic breakthrough in how we think about relationships and about change. The next decade will be exciting. On the one hand, we must not approach it naively. Issues of values, power and ideas must constantly be scrutinized. On the other hand, complexity and evolutionary theories are compellingly convincing that it is in our self-interest to take some risks, to live and learn on the edge of chaos, striking a balance between too much and too little structure. These theories also tell us that systems of interaction and information exchange have self-organizing capacities, which in effect build in checks and balances tantamount to just-in-time monitoring. The self-consciousness of culture can make moral purpose a key driver of self-organization, but the pathways will never be simple. In a word, moral purpose becomes dynamically complex.

Chapter 2

Complexity and the Change Process

Strategy is about marrying ideas and capabilities with intuition and daring.

(Saul, 1997, p. 171)

This chapter is about movement. Although the change process, as I have said, is unpredictable in blueprint terms, there are key insights and ideas that enable us to understand complex processes better, and correspondingly to develop the mindset and instincts to take more effective action. Before getting to these new insights or lessons about complex change there are two additional powerful concepts that we need to add to our thinking — organizations as living systems, and the role of knowledge creation in innovation.

Living Systems

In a study of long-lived companies (companies that were successful for decades and more) De Gues (1997) found that 'the living company' was characterized by much greater sensitivity to the chemistry of people within the organization and to the evolution of and relationships with its external environment. As he says, 'to regard a company as a living entity is a first step toward increasing its life expectancy' (p. 10). This gives deeper meaning to the phrase that people and relationships are critical. It is the quality of the relationships among organizational members, as they evolve, that makes for long-term success. 'Companies die, [says De Gues] because their managers focus on the economic activity of producing goods and services, and they forget that their organizations' true nature is that of a community of humans' (p. 3).

The matter of recreating a prairie, which is discussed by Brown and Eisenhardt (1998), is perhaps an even better example because it captures the notion of organic movement. Brown and Eisenhardt ask what would be the best strategy to recreate a prairie, as it was 200 years ago. Your first response, say the authors, is probably to take a rational planful approach: get a plot of land, compile a list of all the plant and animal members of a prairie ecosystem, obtain samples of the relevant species, plant the seeds, release the animals and cultivate. They call this approach 'assemble'. But they say assembly doesn't work for living systems:

> A prairie is something that grows. It has to start small. It has pieces that interact and build on each other. Once it is 'up and running' the prairie works as a complex system that is dependent on the interaction of the system. (p. 195)

They continue:

> The prairie example illustrates the lessons of trying to create a living thing like an anthill, an ecosystem, or even a business . . . something that does not behave mechanically, but rather something that can change and grow over time . . . living things are grown, not assembled. The various species of a prairie [or an organization] are too interdependent to be assembled in one single, massive act of change. It is not only difficult but impossible to know beforehand how the myriad of components will interact to create the final system. Key to creating a prairie is realizing that it is not a highly controlled, single act of creation, but rather an evolution toward a desired end. (p. 197)

This incidentally is why complex innovations don't spread so easily. To know that collaborative cultures are more effective and even to know how they work tells you almost nothing about how to create one in your own organization (see chapter 3). It is one thing to see an innovation 'up and running', it is entirely another matter to figure out the pathways of how to get there in your own organization. Let me pose and then answer the most frequently noted question when it comes to change. The question asked with more and more frustration is: 'If we know so much about the change process why don't people use this knowledge?' The answer is twofold. One, we have not yet appreciated the organic, evolutionary nature of the processes of human and organizational change — something to which this book attempts to make a contribution; two, as we begin to appreciate these processes, we realize that there can be no cookbooks or silver bullets. Each situation is complex and to a certain degree unique. And, living things grow, adapt and evolve. 'Change is what living things do', say Brown and Eisenhardt (1998). In short, there are no shortcuts or substitutes to living and learning in the rollercoaster of complex change.

Knowledge Creation

So far I have said little explicitly about knowledge. Clearly to talk about a learning organization is to talk about continuously acquiring and using new and better knowledge. Again I must emphasize *movement.* Knowledge creation is not the acquisition of best practices as products. It is the ability to generate and learn new ideas. It is, in other words, a complex change proposition every bit as difficult as anything I have talked about so far. We cannot understand and attempt to harness change forces until we also find a way to increase the capacity to incorporate new ideas. Nonaka and Takeuchi (1995) in their study of successful Japanese companies explain that Japanese companies were not successful due to their manufacturing prowess or human resource practices and the like, but rather because of their skills and expertise at 'organizational knowledge creation', which they define:

> By organizational knowledge creation we mean the capability of a company as a whole to create new knowledge, disseminate it throughout the organization, and embody it in products, services and systems. (p. 3)

It turns out that organizational knowledge creation is a deep but understandable process, and one that is intimately consistent with the theories and findings that I have advanced so far.

Nonaka and Takeuchi make the crucial distinction between explicit knowledge (words and numbers that can be communicated and shared in the form of hard data) and tacit knowledge (skills and beliefs which are below the level of awareness):

> [Japanese companies] recognize that the knowledge expressed in words and numbers represents only the tip of the iceberg. They view knowledge as being primarily 'tacit' — something not easily visible and expressible. Tacit knowledge is highly personal and hard to formalize, making it difficult to communicate or share with others. Subjective insights, intuitions, and hunches fall into this category of knowledge. Furthermore, tacit knowledge is deeply rooted in an individual's action and experience, as well as in the ideals, values, or emotions that he or she embraces. (p. 8)

In brief, the secret to success of living companies, complex adaptive systems, learning communities or whatever terms we wish to use, is that they consist of intricate, embedded interaction inside and outside the organization which *converts tacit knowledge to explicit knowledge on an ongoing basis.*

This is a fantastic insight into how learning takes place in collaborative cultures, and into why formal planning fails. Formal planning is logical and analytical and introduces explicit knowledge, not bad in itself but woefully inadequate. Organizations good at conversion tap into the values, meanings, day-to-day skills, knowledge and experiences of all members of the organization (including the outside-the-organization connection) and make them available for organizational problem-solving. Of course, isolated cultures, like the robin in the titmouse story, have no means of getting at these sources of knowledge and no means of mobilizing the competencies and motivation of organizational members.

The process of knowledge creation is no easy task. First, tacit knowledge by definition is hard to get at. Second, it must sort out and yield quality ideas; not all tacit knowledge is useful. Third, quality ideas must be retained, shared and used throughout the organization.

Thus, the theory of knowledge creation is crucial. As Nonaka and Takeuchi (1995) say:

> The sharing of tacit knowledge among multiple individuals with different backgrounds, perspectives, and motivations becomes the critical step for organizational knowledge creation to take place. The individuals' emotions, feelings, and mental models have to be shared to build mutual trust. (p. 85)

The process of tacit knowledge conversion makes middle managers, like principals, crucial. Neither top-down strategies (they don't get at tacit knowledge) nor bottom-up strategies (they get at but don't convert tacit knowledge into usable, shared explicit knowledge) work. Middle managers can help mediate external and internal forces toward purposeful knowledge creation by attacking incoherence resulting from overloaded and fragmented situations, i.e. the normal situations we find these days on the edge of chaos.

An important caution about knowledge creation is to build in the checks and balances needed to prevent 'groupthink'. Groupthink is when people in a tightly knit culture go along uncritically with the group and/or squelch individual dissent. Tacit knowledge, converted or not into explicit knowledge, can represent prejudices and self-sealing groupthink. This is why a healthy respect for diversity and conflict is essential, along with an openness and learning orientation to the environment and all its variety.

Leonard's (1995) study of knowledge-building activities in successful companies provides additional insights. Citing Chaparral, a highly successful steel company, Leonard identifies four primary learning activities:

> Three of these activities are internally focussed: (1) shared, creative problem solving (to produce current products); (2) implementing and integrating new methodologies and tools (to enhance internal operations); and (3) formal and informal experimentation (to build capabilities for the future) [the externally focussed activity is] (4) pulling in expertise from the outside. (p. 8)

Leonard makes a brilliant distinction among three types of skills and knowledge: (a) public or scientific, (b) industry-specific and (c) firm-specific (p. 21). In Chaparral's industry, the science of metallurgy is public; industry-specific knowledge is available about the manufacture of steel among suppliers and consultants; and 'in-house' (firm-specific) knowledge is in the heads and experiences of employees. The latter of course is none other than tacit knowledge. Leonard's formulation is another contribution toward understanding why the performance of successful organizations cannot be easily duplicated (you can't transfer tacit knowledge) and why the loss of experienced employees in mergers and other transformations is often irreplaceable. In this sense, the goal of organizations on the move includes drawing on outside ideas and expertise, but above all must focus on the growth of firm-specific knowledge among members of the organization — you can't hire firm-specific knowledge, you must grow it (Leonard, 1995, p. 51).

In short, the growth of core capabilities to find and process good ideas is the strength of successful organizations, but it is always problematic and dynamic: 'Knowledge reservoirs in organizations are not static pools but wellsprings, constantly replenished with streams of new ideas and constituting an ever-flowing source of corporate renewal' (Leonard, 1995, p. 3).

Complex Change Lessons

Understanding the dynamics of living systems and knowledge creation allows us to pursue new and more complex change lessons. In the first book, *Change Forces*, I summarized the main insights at the time into eight basic lessons reproduced here:

Lesson One: You Can't Mandate What Matters
(The more complex the change the less you can force it.)

Lesson Two: Change Is a Journey Not a Blueprint
(Change is non-linear, loaded with uncertainty and excitement and sometimes perverse.)

Lesson Three: Problems Are Our Friends
(Problems are inevitable and you can't learn without them.)

Lesson Four: Vision and Strategic Planning Come Later
(Premature visions and planning blind.)

Lesson Five: Individualism and Collectivism Must Have Equal Power
(There are no one-sided solutions to isolation and groupthink.)

Lesson Six: Neither Centralization Nor Decentralization Works
(Both top-down and bottom-up strategies are necessary.)

Lesson Seven: Connection with the Wider Environment Is Critical for Success
(The best organizations learn externally as well as internally.)

Lesson Eight: Every Person Is a Change Agent
(Change is too important to leave to the experts, personal mind set and mastery is the ultimate protection.) (Fullan, 1993, pp. 21–2)

These lessons still hold, but the theoretical and empirical advances over the past five years have provided a much deeper and more coherent basis for understanding and acting in complex change situations. The new lessons, already alluded to and to be pursued in subsequent chapters, are summarized in Figure 2.1.

Figure 2.1 Complex change lessons

Lesson 1: Moral Purpose Is Complex and Problematic
Lesson 2: Theories of Change and Theories of Education Need Each Other
Lesson 3: Conflict and Diversity Are Our Friends
Lesson 4: Understand the Meaning of Operating on the Edge of Chaos
Lesson 5: Emotional Intelligence Is Anxiety Provoking and Anxiety Containing
Lesson 6: Collaborative Cultures Are Anxiety Provoking and Anxiety Containing
Lesson 7: Attack Incoherence: Connectedness and Knowledge Creation Are Critical
Lesson 8: There Is No Single Solution: Craft Your Own Theories and Actions by Being a Critical Consumer

Lesson 1: Moral Purpose Is Complex and Problematic

Moral purpose is complex because it involves altering the power structure, because it is exceedingly difficult to make the changes necessary
to motivate and support scores of individual students and teachers, and
because moral purpose not only includes academic achievement, but
also must find ways of motivating alienated students and families.

Lesson 1 says be inspired by moral purpose, but don't be naive
about it. Moral purpose must be assisted by the other seven lessons
which can combine to provide the infrastructure and resources necessary to make headway in very difficult terrain.

The politics of moral purpose can also help. Oakes *et al.* (1998)
remind us that while top-down change doesn't work, we still need the
force of top-down mandates. To clarify Lesson 1 in the original *Change
Forces* (You Can't Mandate What Matters) — it is true that you can't
mandate local commitment and capacity, but mandates do matter. They
put needed pressure on local reform, and they provide opportunities
for legitimizing the efforts of local change agents working against the
grain. Top-down mandates and bottom-up energies need each other.
One thing that has changed in the past five years is the sense of urgency
about school reform, and the realization that individual school reform
will never add up to large-scale reform. We are now beginning to see
some of the fruits of more forceful top-down/bottom-up strategies, in
Chicago (Bryk *et al.*, 1998a) and in New York (Elmore and Burney,
1998), for example. Policy initiatives that combine rigorous external
accountability and mechanisms for focusing on local capacity development are critical for success (see chapter 4).

It is necessary also to consider more sophisticated strategies for
students in disadvantaged situations, in particular applying what we
know about student motivation and resilience. With all the interest in
accountability and academic achievement, good intentions can easily
backfire. I would hypothesize that the greater the emphasis on academic achievement through high stakes accountability, the greater the
gap becomes between advantaged and disadvantaged students. The
main reason for this is that poor performing students do not need more
pressure, they need greater attachment to the school and motivation to
want to learn. Pressure by itself in this situation actually demotivates
poor performing students.

The Child Development Project is a good example of combining
an emphasis on academic achievement with a focus on social support
that motivates students (Lewis *et al.*, 1998). CDP is an intervention that
consists of three components; a classroom program (instructionally

focused with student involvement), a school-wide program (fostering student participation and development of values such as helpfulness, responsibility, understanding of others) and a family involvement program (making school welcoming to families and promoting home activities). The approach to change is to provide materials, assistance and support for developing local capacity to implement the three program components. An evaluation study of twelve schools in six districts, found that (a) despite strong external support only about half the schools showed widespread implementation — thereby confirming the difficulty of school-wide reform, and (b) those schools that did accomplish implementation 'significantly increased in a number of resilience-related outcomes and academic attitudes, including attachment to school, intrinsic academic motivation, preference for challenging tasks, frequency of reading outside school, democratic values, intrinsic prosocial motivation, and conflict resolution skills' compared to matched non-program schools (Lewis *et al.*, 1998, p. 1). In other words, moral purpose and change strategies combined to promote greater attachment to the school and greater academic achievement. What we need, then, are even larger-scale efforts where whole districts, whole states, whole nations engage in strategies that simultaneously work on motivation and attachment along with academic achievement. And they must do so, realizing the enormity of the task and the multiyear commitment needed.

Lesson 2: Theories of Education and Theories of Change Need Each Other

There is a valuable but slippery distinction between a theory of education and a theory of change. Although the distinction is not absolutely pure, it is useful to examine change efforts in terms of their theories of education, i.e. what pedagogical assumptions and associated components are essential to the model, and their theories of change or action, i.e. what strategies are formed to guide and support implementation. Many reformers with well worked-out theories of education are nonplussed to find that their valuable ideas are ignored or misused in practice. The first observation is that strategies strong on both sets of theories are more likely to experience success. Stokes *et al.* (1997) found that to be the case in comparing several intervention models including the Child Development Project, which got high marks for having both an education and a change or action theory (and was more successful at getting results). Any good ideas or programs that hope to spread must include in their theories of action, a focus on context.

Local context (readiness to learn, local capacity, etc.) is a crucial variable, and no program can expect to spread successfully if it does not take into account the various contexts which it will inevitably encounter.

A related observation is how important it is to work at making explicit the theories of action (change) that underlay the models of change. Hatch (1998) did just that in his examination of the ATLAS endeavor — a collaboration of the Coalition of Essential Schools, Education Development Center, Harvard Project Zero and School Development Program. Although the theories of education across the projects were compatible, Hatch found that the four partners had very different theories of action which led to conflicts around three dilemmas of schooling, namely:

> (a) how to establish wide support for improvement efforts and foster innovations that often conflict with conventional expectations; (b) how to balance the needs and interests of students and teachers and the demands of the society in the design of the curricula; and (c) how to allow individuals, schools, and communities the freedom to develop as they see fit while providing sufficient support and direction to ensure that specific outcomes are achieved. (Hatch, 1998, p. 5)

Different approaches to handling these three dilemmas made it extremely difficult to make action decisions to carry out the collaborative work necessary for school improvement. Hatch concludes:

> Rather than trying to forge a single, common theory of action, those involved in reform efforts might be better off trying to gain a deep, respectful understanding of when and why they are likely to disagree. (p. 25)

The third and most profound observation is that there never will be a definitive theory of change. It is a theoretical and empirical impossibility to generate a theory that applies to all situations. Definitive theories of change are unknowable because they do not and cannot exist. Theories of change can guide thinking and action, as I attempt to do in this book, but the reality of complexity tells us that each situation will have degrees of uniqueness in its history and makeup which will cause unpredictable differences to emerge.

Fourth and finally, it is the task of change theorists and practitioners to accumulate their wisdom and experience about how the change process works. Sometimes this will be model-specific insights of change, i.e. the best approaches to implement aspects of a given model. All times it will be discipline-based (change as a discipline) ideas such as those contained in the eight lessons. In this respect, Lesson 3 is a great, new example.

Lesson 3: Conflict and Diversity Are Our Friends

Problems used to be our friends in *Change Forces*, but this lesson has gone deeper to find that it is differences and conflict that are even greater friends. Conflict, if respected, is positively associated with creative breakthroughs under complex, turbulent conditions. Consensus would be pleasant, but actually is impossible to achieve except through superficial agreement. As Stacey (1996b) observes:

> The creative process in human systems . . . is inevitably messy: it involves differences, conflict, fantasy, and emotion; it stirs up anger, envy, depression, and many other feelings. To remove the mess by inspiring us to follow some common vision, share the same culture, and pull together is to remove the mess that is the very raw material of creative activity. (p. 15)

De Gues (1997) found that 'long-lived companies were tolerant' of differences: 'These companies were particularly tolerant of activities on the margin: outliers, experiments, and eccentricities' (p. 7). The studies of knowledge-creating companies draw the same conclusion: 'The sharing of tacit knowledge among multiple individuals *with different backgrounds, perceptions, and motivations*' is the first critical step (Nonaka and Takeuchi, 1995, p. 85, my italics).

Similarly, Leonard (1995) talks about the value of 'creative abrasion': 'Some managers of innovative organizations select people *because* their ideas, biases, personalities, values, and skills conflict — not in spite of their differences' (p. 63, italics in original). Organizations, of course, that promote ethnic, culture, gender and other inclusionary policies as well as global partnerships across cultures build in natural sources of diversity.

It is not diversity *per se* that counts but 'collaborative' diversity. And collaborative diversity means conflict. Homogeneous cultures may have little disagreement, but they are also less interesting. Heterogeneous cultures risk greater conflict, but they also contain stronger seeds of breakthrough. As Maurer (1996) observes, 'resistance' is an essential ingredient of progress.

Often those who resist have something important to tell us. We can be influenced by them. People resist for what they view as good reasons. They may see alternatives we never dreamed of. They may understand problems about the minutiae of implementation that we never see from our lofty perch atop Mount Olympus. (p. 49)

As we said in *What's Worth Fighting For Out There?*, 'respecting those you wish to silence' is a good rule of thumb (Hargreaves and Fullan, 1998; Heifetz, 1994). You often learn more from people who disagree with you than you do from people who agree, but you underlisten to the former and overlisten to the latter. You associate with people who agree with you, and you avoid those with whom you disagree. Not a good learning strategy. Incidentally, this is the main reason why the strategy of going with like-minded innovators is shortsighted. Elmore (1995, p. 20) puts it this way: 'Small groups of self-selected reformers apparently seldom influence their peers.' They just create an even greater gap between themselves and others, which eventually becomes impossible to bridge. In other words, it is better to incorporate differences early in the process of change (when there is a chance to address problems) than to avoid conflict only to have to face it later when it is unresolvable. In complexity theory terms, if you avoid differences you may enjoy early smoothness, but you pay the price because you do not get at the really difficult issues until it is too late.

Thus another lesson and another reason that change is complex is that to be effective you have to form relationships with people you might not understand and might not like (or vice versa). Working through the discomfort of each other's presence, learning from dissonance, and forging new more complex agreements and capabilities is a new requirement for living on the edge of chaos.

Lesson 4: Understand the Meaning of Operating on the Edge of Chaos

Living on the edge of chaos means getting used to a certain degree of uncertainty:

> The underlying argument is that when systems of any kind (e.g., beehives, businesses, economies) are poised on the edge of chaos between too much structure and too little structure, they 'self-organize' to produce complex adaptive behaviour. If there were more structure, then these systems would be too rigid to move. If there were less structure, then they would fly apart chaotically. (Brown and Eisenhardt, 1998, p. 29)

To understand living on the edge of chaos definitely does not mean accepting anarchy. Really chaotic systems have no direction, unclear responsibilities, random communication, limited purposeful experimentation and consequently *no learning*. By contrast the edge of chaos has both structure and openendedness. Elements of structure include the guidance of moral purpose, a small number of key priorities and a focus on knowledge and data arising from shared problem-solving and assessment of results. According to Brown and Eisenhardt (1998, p. 47), the management practices for navigating the edge of chaos involve the need to:

- foster a culture of frequent change in the context of a few strict rules;
- keep most activity loosely structured but rely on critical structure points of priorities, targeted measures, real deadlines and responsibilities for major outcomes;
- create channels for real-time fact-based communication within and across groups.

How do complex systems 'self-organize' — a key concept in chaos theory? Periodic consolidation and self-organizing patterns are inevitable because the process is driven by (a) intense interaction and communication, (b) knowledge-creation in relation to selected problems, and (c) a value system — moral purpose in our terms — that knows a good outcome when it sees it.

Lesson 4 in summary is: do not try to micromanage change through lots of rules, rigid structures and formal channels of communication (Brown and Eisenhardt, 1998, p. 41). Rather, set up a system of people-based learning framed by a few key priorities and structures. The hard part is taking the risk to *trust* the process as you embed it in complexity theory and the lessons of change contained in this chapter. And remember, while this is theory — deep theory in many ways — it is based on the studies of actual organizations which have outperformed all others. Effective organizations do trust the process, but not completely; they design their work in a way that is not left up to chance (see chapters 3 and 4).

Lesson 5: Emotional Intelligence Is Anxiety Provoking and Anxiety Containing

People with moral purpose in troubled times know that a certain amount of anxiety in themselves and others is necessary, even valuable.

Complexity creates change. Change means facing the unknown. Facing the unknown means anxiety. Naturally we want to reduce anxiety, but there are good and bad ways of containing anxiety. Stacey (1996b) observes:

> . . . denial of uncertainty itself allows us to sustain the fantasy of someone up there being in control and, perhaps, of things turning out for the best if we simply do what we are told, and so it protects us for a while from anxiety. However, because that defensive response involves dependency and a flight from reality, it hardly ever works. (pp. 7–8)

Similarly, Heifetz (1994, p. 37), in *Leadership Without Easy Answers*, says:

> . . . people fail to adapt because of the stress provoked by the problem and the changes it demands. They resist the pain, anxiety or conflict that accompanies a sustained interaction with the situation. Holding onto past assumptions, blaming authority, scapegoating, externalizing the enemy, denying the problem, jumping to conclusions, or finding a distracting issue may resolve stability and feel less stressful than facing and taking responsibility for a complex challenge.

Anxiety, as Stacey (1996b, p. 188) concludes, is 'an inevitable feature of mental life at the edge of chaos; the ability to bear that anxiety is a prerequisite for dwelling there.' Emotionally intelligent people handle anxiety better. Whether one takes the five domains identified by Goleman (1995) — knowing one's emotions, managing emotions, motivating oneself, empathy and interpersonal effectiveness — or some other variation, emotionally intelligent people live longer and better, and they don't do it by avoiding anxiety. They are better able to find solitude when necessary, seek support from and give help to others, persist in the face of challenges, identify with and are sustained by a higher goal (moral purpose) and so on. Emotional intelligence at work is absolutely crucial for effectiveness in complex environments. The evidence is overwhelming (Goleman, 1998).

Heifetz (1994) elaborates:

> . . . people adapt more successfully to their environments, given their purposes and values, by facing painful circumstances and developing new attitudes and behaviors. They learn to distinguish reality from fantasy, resolve internal conflicts and put harsh events into perspective. They learn to live with things that cannot be changed and take responsibility for those that can. By improving their ability to reflect,

strengthening their tolerance for frustration, and understanding their own blind spots and patterns of resistance to facing problems, they improve their general adaptive capacity for future challenge.

Lesson 5, in effect, is: work on developing a stronger ego structure not by avoiding anxiety, but by seeking and containing it within creative bounds.

Lesson 6: Collaborative Cultures Are Anxiety Provoking and Anxiety Containing

Closely related is the dual role of collaborative cultures. On the one hand, collaboration to be effective must foster a degree of difference. In talking about 'creative abrasion' Leonard (1995, p. 63) says that managers of innovative organizations often select people with different ideas:

> Why? Because an effective guard against people's considering only a few problem-solving alternatives or worse, framing problems so that they can be solved only with familiar solutions, is to involve a variety of people, with diverse signature skills, in the task. As different ideas rub against each other, sparks fly. However, in a well-managed process, the sparks are creative, not personal.

In leadership terms the challenge is to develop and support people's capacity 'for tackling an ongoing stream of hard problems' (Heifetz, 1994, p. 247). If anxiety is firmly contained by bureaucracy, hierarchy and/or dependence on the leader, the level of stress drops, but the ability to solve complex problems also diminishes.

Thus, on the other hand, collaborative cultures must go about their business of anxiety-related experimentation and problem-solving by providing 'a good enough holding environment':

> It is not simply the extent of connectivity but the quality of the connections that causes the system to operate at the edge. So if relationships have the quality of trust and compassion, if they are based on empathy and love, then they operate as very effective containers of anxiety. Given high quality interconnectedness, a group can contain anxiety and stay at the edge of chaos. (Stacey, 1996b, p. 162)

In their comparison of healthy families and healthy organizations, Skynner and Cleese (1993, p. 32) observe that it is the 'degree of emotional support' that family or organization members can draw on 'which mainly accounts for the ease with which they deal with change.' Effective individuals and organizations recognize that anxiety always accompanies change, and they are more confident that they can handle it.

In short, vitality springs from experiencing conflict and tension in systems which also incorporate anxiety-containing supportive relationships. Collaborative cultures are innovative not just because they provide support, but also because they recognize the value of dissonance inside and outside the organization.

Lesson 7: Attack Incoherence: Connectedness and Knowledge Creation Are Critical

With change forces abounding, it is easy to experience overload, fragmentation and incoherence. In fact, in education this is the more typical state. Policies get passed independent of each other, innovations are introduced before previous ones are adequately implemented, the sheer presence of problems and multiple unconnected solutions are overwhelming. Many schools and school systems make matters worse by indiscriminately taking on every innovation that comes along — what Bryk *et al.* (1998a) called 'Christmas tree schools' — so many innovations as decorations, superficially adorned.

Since the natural state in complex societies is confusion, it follows that those who are successful vigorously work at meaning-making. Neither top-down nor bottom-up strategies by themselves can achieve coherence — the top is too distant and the bottom is overwhelmed. This is why Nonaka and Takeuchi (1995, p. 128) conclude that middle managers (e.g. principals) are essential as integrators and synthesizers. This is why Bryk *et al.* (1998a) found that the Chicago schools who were most effective had principals who helped staff 'attack incoherence, make connections, and focussed on continuity from one program to another.'

We can also see why guided knowledge creation procedures are essential. The conversion of tacit knowledge to explicit knowledge is a meaning-making proposition because it brings knowledge out into the open to be shared. Similarly, the use of evaluation data arising from experiments or otherwise serves this same coherence-making function. When data on the performance of the company or the school are made available, and when collaborative cultures examine these data in order to make changes based on the information, they become clearer about how well they are doing. Indeed, they become more clear about their values, goals and what they should be doing.

Coherence doesn't happen by accident, and doesn't happen by pursuing everything under the sun. Effective organizations are not ones that innovate the most; they are not ones that send personnel on the most number of staff development conferences. No, they are organizations that *selectively* go about learning more. In all of their activities, even ones that foster diversity, they create mechanisms of integration. Moral purpose, communication, intense interaction, implementation plans, performance data all serve the purpose of coherence. In examining new policies or possibilities integrative organizations not only worry about the value of each opportunity, but they also ask how the new idea 'connects' with what they are doing. Shared meaning and organizational connectedness are the long-term assets of high performing systems.

Lesson 8: There Is No Single Solution: Craft Your Own Theories and Actions by Being a Critical Consumer

The previous seven lessons in combination should make it abundantly clear once and for all, why there never can be a silver bullet of change. The change process is too intricate and organic, organization by organization, to be captured in any single model. Yet there is great vulnerability to packaged solutions because the change process is so nerve-wracking.

Even when you know what research and published advice has to say you will not know exactly how to apply it to your particular situation with its unique problems, and opportunities. Your own organization has its own special combination of personalities and prehistories, and 'firm-specific' realities. You can get ideas, insights and lines of thought and action, but you can never know exactly how to proceed. Mintzberg (1994, p. 27) puts the problem in an interesting way:

> Never adopt a technique by its usual name. If you want to do re-engineering or whatever, call it something different so that you have to think it through for yourself and work it out on your own terms. If you just adopt it and implement it, it is bound to fail.

The only shortcuts available turn out to be roads to superficiality and dependency. Once you realize that these roads have no chance of leading anywhere — in fact you lose ground as everyone knows the organization is going nowhere — it can be quite liberating. As the bonds of dependency are broken, it turns out that there are tremendous resources available — ideas, partnerships, expertise inside and outside the organization, etc.

As you follow a process of continually converting your tacit knowledge about change into explicit change knowledge, refining and marrying it with insights from the change literature, you begin to craft your own theories of change. You become a critical consumer of innovation and reform as you increase your capacity to 'manage' the change process, including tolerance of certain degrees of uncertainty, and greater trust that if you have the right ingredients things will work out more times than not. Ultimately, Lesson 8 says that no one can solve your change problems but yourself.

A Final Note

Following any one lesson independently of the others would be misleading. The eight lessons only have power in combination. There is no point celebrating diversity and conflict if you are not also working on connectedness and coherence. There is little to be gained by having a theory of change unless moral purpose is front and center. You can't craft viable theories of action unless you are heavily engaged in living and learning from the previous seven lessons, and so on. As these lessons are internalized, the reward is that they can become an indispensable guide to thinking about and acting effectively in the face of complex and chaotic change.

As we reflect on these lessons and the theories of complexity and evolution that I have put forth so far, it is fair to ask a series of questions. Is there evidence that certain strategies fail because they do not address the ideas I have identified? What do reform strategies that acknowledge chaos and complexity look like? Is there evidence of their success?

First, almost everyone would agree (although they have different views on what or whom to blame) that previous reform strategies have failed. I maintain that these failures have occurred because the theories of change underpinning them are simplistic or absent altogether. Top-down strategies cause grief but no relief. Bottom-up approaches produce the odd spurt but eventually drown in a sea of inertia.

Second, we don't fully know what strategies based on complexity and chaos will look like in education reform, partly because we are at the early stage of these new discoveries and largely because educational systems operate too much like political bureaucracies. They seemingly dwell in chaos, but they do not purposefully live and learn on the *creative* edge of chaos. They have not yet proven capable of balancing 'too much and too little structure' on the way to continuous learning.

Third, while we don't know what these strategies would 'fully' entail, we are now seeing more sophisticated examples in operation in public school systems. And, there is early evidence of their success. Further, these education-specific strategies are entirely consistent with the concepts and insights arising from complexity and evolutionary theory. Chapters 3 to 5 present these exciting findings and give us ideas and hope for the future.

In the remaining chapters the ideas behind the lessons should become more and more meaningful. In chapter 3, I examine why collaboration inside the organization is essential, what its deeper nature is and why it gets the results it does. In chapter 4, I take up similar ideas in considering why effective organizations must have two-way collaborative relationships with the outside. Chapter 5 looks into another perplexing facet of the problem of change — why transferability, large-scale reform and dissemination run into so many problems. Finally, chapter 6 considers the multiplying energy of combining strategies that simultaneously draw on ideas, power and purpose. Fusing these intellectual, political and spiritual forces may be our best bet for coping with the challenge of complexity that pervades our daily lives.

Chapter 3

The Deep Meaning of Inside Collaboration

Holding organizational anxiety requires [an] internal container. The internal container is provided by a culture of trust and particular patterns of power use.

(Stacey, 1996b, p. 189)

Are schools so fundamentally different from business firms that any comparisons are misleading? Certainly in one sense they are in similar predicaments — their environments are tumultuous, uncertain and increasingly intrusive. They are different perhaps in two basic ways; one is an asset, the other a liability. The asset, as we have seen, is that education is much more explicitly and deeply a moral enterprise, providing schools with an inspirational mandate of a higher order. The liability, compared to businesses, is that school systems are mired in inertial bureaucracy. For this latter reason many have concluded that transforming public schools is hopeless. If these critics are to be proven wrong, one reason will pertain to how schools can become collaborative learning organizations.

The Black Box of Collaboration

We and others have written that collaborative schools (or the more popular phrase these days, professional learning communities) are essential for success (Fullan and Hargreaves, 1992). The study of school restructuring by Newmann and Wehlage (1995) and their colleagues Louis and Kruse (1995) provides the most explicit evidence on the relationship between professional community and student performance. Using measures of standardized achievement tests and more 'authentic' performance-based measures of learning, these researchers found that some schools did much better (using student achievement in mathematics, science and social sciences as the indicators). They trace the reasons for this better performance to whether or not the school had a 'high professional community'.

Figure 3.1   The nature of professional learning communities. (Adapted from Newmann and Wehlage, 1995, and Louis and Kruse, 1995.)

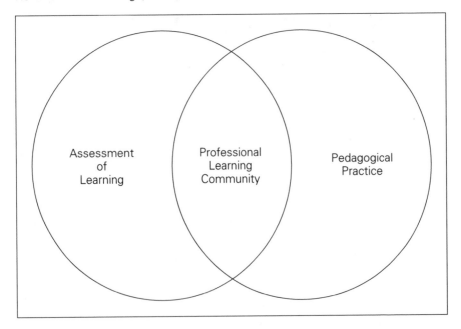

In essence, their argument about the internal workings of successful schools is that professional communities make the difference because, in their words:

- Teachers pursue a clear purpose for all students' learning.
- Teachers engage in collaborative activity to achieve the purpose.
- Teachers take collaborative responsibility for student learning . . . [And]
- Schoolwide teacher professional community affected the level of classroom authentic pedagogy, which in turn affected student performance.
- Schoolwide teacher professional community affected the level of social support for student learning, which in turn affected student performance. (Newmann and Wehlage, 1995, pp. 30, 32)

In one sense, Newmann and Wehlage and Louis and Kruse are the first to uncover 'the black box' of collaborative schools, which I have depicted in Figure 3.1.

What happens in these schools is that teachers as a group and as subgroups examine together how well students are doing (i.e. they study student work and assessment data), they relate this to how they are teaching (i.e. to instructional practice), and they make continuous refinements individually and with each other (i.e. as a professional community). By contrast, in individualistic or balkanized cultures, teachers either leave each other alone or are at loggerheads — disagreeing without any inclination or process to solve differences.

Newmann and colleagues should be congratulated for going deeper than anyone else. We can now imagine, if not see, some of the inner workings of collaborative schools. We have peered inside the black box. But, from a change or movement point of view, there is one fundamental way in which these findings remain relatively superficial. The black box turns out to contain attractive ingredients, but not much help about how to use them. The reader can do a small test at this point. Go back to Figure 3.1 and become convinced that the synergy of the three ingredients would indeed produce results. Now, ask yourself what you would do on Monday morning in your school or district to produce such a system. My prediction is that you will not have very clear ideas about what pathways to follow.

The reason for this is twofold (and now we start to go deeper in relation to the complexity of change processes). First, Newmann and colleagues examined successful schools that were already 'up and running.' They did not study how they got that way. This is the limitation of cross-sectional studies that provide a snapshot or portrayal of what is out there. They do not and cannot capture movement. How to get there remains in the black box. It is useful, then, to treat as problematic the question of 'how' to go about chang*ing* (to be fair, Newmann and colleagues did identify other factors related to success internal to the school (e.g. leadership) and external to the school (e.g. standards and staff development), but these also were already 'up and running'). *Changing* remains problematic.

Deeper still, as I said in Lesson 8 (chapter 2), even if we had longitudinal studies of how other organizations have transformed successfully, this would fall short of what we need to do in our own particular school-specific situation. This, as I concluded earlier, can never be answered definitively. What we can do, however, is to probe the deeper dynamics of the nature of collaborative organizations. This will lead to better insights and more sophisticated understandings that will help us craft more productive strategies and actions.

I will use two more examples before drawing conclusions about the deep meaning of inside collaboration. One example comes from our work in secondary school reform in Winnipeg with the Gordon Foundation (1998) in the Manitoba School Improvement Program (MSIP).

MSIP is a program designed to improve secondary schools in Manitoba: 'To improve the learning experiences and outcomes of secondary school students, particularly those at risk, by building schools' capacities to become transforming schools that engage students actively in their own learning.' Multiyear grants are provided to schools for self-directed improvement initiatives. Over twenty schools have been funded over the past seven years. Using a school improvement index composed of measures of student learning, student engagement, school improvement processes and project success, the external evaluators found that many schools improved, some quite substantially (Earl and Lee, 1998).

Earl and Lee further unpack the 'black box' of collaboration by suggesting that success is a function of urgency–agency–energy. In unsuccessful schools any sense of urgency (e.g. dying to make a difference or moral purpose) that teachers have turns to despair as they struggle with the cognitive and emotional dissonance of repeated frustration. In schools with a combination of internal (this chapter) and external (chapter 4) pressure and support, not only is the sense of urgency endorsed and aroused, it is aided and abetted by the agency of collaboration, more precisely the kinds of collaborative cultures that focus on learning, provoke and contain anxiety, pursue ongoing inquiry and reflection, and work towards cumulative coherence. As Earl and Lee (1998) argue, urgency and agency together generate more energy leading to consolidation, reflection, celebration and the capacity to push even deeper in a further spiral of reform activity.

The Chicago reform story, which we will look at more fully in chapter 4 as an example of system reform, is equally instructive about the dynamics of individual school improvement. Chicago began an experiment in 1988 that dramatically changed the power and authority at the local level in its 550 schools (Bryk *et al.*, 1998a). In this chapter I consider only the question of individual school success. Bryk *et al.* (1998b) report that for elementary schools (not secondary schools) learning gains in reading and mathematics improved substantially in the recent years of the reform. In value added terms, comparing 1996 with 1994 the gains ranged from 10 to 40 per cent on average. Some schools, over one-third, improved substantially, others improved moderately, whereas a minority (some 15 per cent) declined.

Bryk *et al.* (1998a) provide further detail for our black box explanation. They say that staff who are better prepared for the inevitable 'confusion and conflict associated with organizational change' fare better (p. 32). Their summary of the salient features of organizational change sounds familiar:

- Engagement of parents and community resources;
- Access to new ideas;
- Professional community;
- Internalizing responsibility for change;
- Strategic educational planning (working towards coherence). (Bryk *et al.*, 1998a, pp. 127–9)

Five years into the reform about one-third (some 156 of the 473) of the elementary schools were engaged in 'self-initiating, actively restructuring' processes:

These schools appeared headed in a productive direction. Substantial social resources had formed. Supportive relationships existed both within the professional staff and with parents and the local community. A palpable sense of both urgency and agency had emerged: 'We can make a difference for our children and we must do this.' Better conditions had also been created for improvements in classroom teaching — long-needed instructional materials had been purchased, new ideas had been introduced, new strategies were being tried, and support for change was now being offered by school leadership, and a wide-range of outside organizations and individual agents. In essence, the table was set for the continued efforts that would be needed to significantly improve student learning. If these schools stayed on course, such results seemed likely. (Bryk *et al.*, 1998a, p. 262)

Interestingly, this prediction, based on findings up to 1994, has since proven accurate as 1996 student achievement data show substantial gains in one-third or more of the schools (Bryk *et al.*, 1998b). It seems almost certain that the schools who showed achievement gains by 1996 were by and large the ones positioned to do so by 1994.

The three key concepts of local school reform in Chicago according to Bryk *et al.* (1998a, p. 206) are (a) the politics of increasing participation and democracy, (b) a focus on systemic restructuring through school improvement planning and (c) innovative instruction.

In a related paper on school leadership, Sebring and Bryk (1998) elaborate. Principals in successful schools take 'a long-term focus on instructional core', 'use the School Improvement Plan' to bring participants into a process of developing a comprehensive plan, and 'attack incoherence'. They work hard at 'connectedness' because they know that fragmentation, overload, and incoherence are endemic problems. They work effectively with staff to achieve greater coherence in the face of disjointed innovations in the external environment.

Bryk *et al.* (1998a) warn, as I did earlier, that despite some clear and convincing findings, complex change does not unfold in a linear fashion: 'These developments are intricately tied to the peculiarities of each school context; not only its prior work on restructuring, but also its longer term social history' (p. 211).

Bryk *et al.* (1998a) found that the Chicago schools that made a difference worked differently internally as 'professional communities' of teachers discussed and acted on new ideas:

> In schools making systemic changes, structures are established which create opportunities for such interactions to occur. As teachers develop a broader say in school decision making, they may also begin to experiment with new roles, including working collaboratively. This restructuring of teachers' work signifies a broadening professional community where teachers feel more comfortable exchanging ideas, and where a collective sense of responsibility for student development is likely to emerge. These characteristics of systemic restructuring contrast with conventional school practice where teachers work more autonomously, and there may be little meaningful professional exchange among co-workers. (p. 128)

In summary, there are two basic conclusions to be made about the black box of collaborative cultures. First, it is a black box and therefore we must examine its dynamic contents more carefully in order to get a better understanding of what is happening. Second, even if we better understand the black boxes of other organizations, it will not precisely tell us what to do in our own situation. The particular pathways are always to a certain extent unique because of the ecology of living systems.

What gives us confidence that we are on the right track, however, is how the deeper theoretical meaning of collaborative work is beginning to make so much sense.

The Deep Meaning of Inside Collaboration

Figure 3.2 summarizes the key characteristics of 'collaborative cultures for complex times'. It provides, I think, a deeper and more sophisticated theoretical understanding of why certain schools (organizations) do so well. And while it reveals why it is specifically impossible to imitate such successes, it does inspire more powerful insight and action.

First, contrary to myth, effective collaborative cultures are not based on like-minded consensus. They value diversity because that is how

Figure 3.2 Characteristics of collaborative cultures for complex times

- Fosters diversity while trust-building
- Provokes anxiety and contains it
- Engages in knowledge creation (tacit to explicit, explicit to explicit)
- Combines connectedness with openendedness
- Fuses the spiritual, political and intellectual

they get different perspectives and access to ideas to address complex problems. Under such conditions, inequity is far less likely to go unnoticed or to be tolerated. At the same time, conflict is brought out into the open. There is a great deal of team-building, diverse groups working together, and intense communication and information sharing. There are a small number of integrative structures — key priorities, mechanisms for planning and problem-solving and a focus on core outcomes. A tolerance for experimentation and making mistakes is coupled with intense interaction. On the problem-solving side:

> It is true dialogue in which people engage with each other, not to be in control but to provoke and be provoked, to learn and contribute to the learning of others, to change their own minds as well as the minds of others. (Stacey, 1996b, p. 280)

On the community-building side, these schools and organizations know that the quality of relationships is central to success. Success is only possible if organizational members develop trust and compassion for each other, i.e. for others different than themselves (given that diversity is built in). If you understand the deep meaning of achieving diversity *and* community building, you avoid fatal mistakes. Instead of going only with like-minded innovators, or investing only in newcomers, you are more likely to foster creative mixes. Brown and Eisenhardt (1998, p. 122) advise: 'Try putting experienced people in your new opportunities. At a minimum, build in incentives for experienced staff to help new people, and for the new people to solicit and use their colleagues' help.'

Second, diversity, openendedness and relentlessly pursuing highly complex problems all provoke personal and group anxiety and conflict. Emotions until recently were thought to be a diversion or barrier to problem-solving. New research and insights on the role of emotions are destroying popular assumptions that emotions cloud logic. Damasio (1994) observes that 'an important [and erroneous] aspect of the rationalist conception is that to obtain the best results, emotions must be kept *out.* Rational processing must be unencumbered by passion' (p. 171, italics in original). Emotions, says Damasio, are actually indispensable to rational decision-making. People who are emotionally flat might be able to perform abstract intellectual tasks, but they can't make practical judgments of human value:

> In real life, a purely logical search through all possibilities is not possible (because of limitations of resources, multiple goals, and problems of coordination with others). Nevertheless, we must act . . . despite our limitations we must take responsibility for our actions, and suffer their effects. This is why emotions or something like them are necessary to bridge across the unexpected and the unknown, to guide reason, and to give priorities among multiple goals. (Oatley and Jenkins, 1996, p. 123)

Collaborative organizations fan the passion and emotions of its members because they so value commitment and the energy required to pursue complex goals. But instead of leaving passionate teachers to sink or swim, the true value of collaborative cultures is that they simultaneously encourage passion and provide emotional support as people work through the rollercoaster of change. In this sense these organizations foment moral purpose while providing support for its pursuit.

Third, stirring the emotions and motivating people and even encouraging people who are already motivated is not sufficient. Also needed are quality *ideas* — knowledge, expertise and the continuous development of best practices. To understand the nature and power of collaborative cultures is to know that they function to access the tacit knowledge of all organizational members (thereby making it explicit) while also seeking new ideas and knowledge available in the world outside. This knowledge creation process is central to success. When teachers in the Newmann and Wehlage (1995) schools sit down together and study student work, when they relate this student performance to how they are teaching, and when they get better ideas from each other and from best practice outside to improve their teaching practices, they are engaged in a knowledge creation process that is absolutely essential. When the successful schools in Chicago are progressing, they access each other's knowledge:

> [Teachers] go in and teach each other's classes and see how each other works. One of the first things they learned was that each person had somewhat different expertise and could be a real resource for each other. If they felt comfortable with something they had observed, they were going to go back and try it in their classrooms. (Bryk *et al.*, 1998a, p. 238)

Fourth, the biggest problem facing schools is fragmentation and overload. It is worse for schools than for business firms. Both are facing turbulent and uncertain environments, but only schools are suffering the additional burden of having a torrent of unwanted, uncoordinated policies and innovations raining down on them from external hierarchical bureaucracies. For all the reasons stated so far, collaborative schools are in a better position to work on connectedness under these conditions. As we saw, the best Chicago schools integrate innovations into school improvement plans. When new ideas or policies come along they ask not only whether the idea is potentially good for them, but also how they can integrate it with what they are already working on. These schools are concerned about cumulative continuity, and because they have a growing conception of what they are looking for (a conception of improved performance deriving from the clarity of knowledge creation and internalization and driven by data) they do achieve greater coherence. This is noteworthy because they achieve this coherence even when the policy environment is fragmentary.

It is important to remind ourselves that collaborative schools are not necessarily the most innovative — they are *selectively* innovative. It is enticing in today's marketplace to make the mistake of Bryk *et al.*'s 'Christmas tree schools':

> [These schools] engaged in aggressive efforts to bring many new programs and services to their schools. Much less attention, however, focused on quality implementation of these initiatives or on how well each new option related to what was already in place. The overall effect was the proliferation of weakly implemented and unaligned progress that might make a school look good to the casual observer, but often left staff frustrated and discouraged by the failure to realize significant improvements in student learning. (p. 287)

Again, fundamentally and theoretically it is no accident that collaborative schools with their intense interaction, high-quality information and moral guidance have self-organizing capacities. Leaders are essential but at the same time teachers spontaneously self-organize. Bryk *et al.* (1998a, p. 240) describe what happens at one school when some teachers have learned something valuable at an outside workshop:

> The teachers [when they came back] will just call a meeting on their own, just to get together to share these ideas. *No one is directing this.* We have learned something that may be helpful, and we should share it. (italics in original)

Teachers in these schools, as they work on coherence, have a healthy respect for the openendedness required to thrive in complex environments. They constantly seek and assess external ideas. To become complacent is to become vulnerable. As Andrew Grove (1996), the CEO of Intel, said (with some exaggeration), 'Only the Paranoid Survive'. Thus, collaborative schools operating in rapidly changing situations know that coherence can never be achieved once and for all. Internal membership changes, new threats and opportunities intrude. Coherence-making is thus a never-ending dynamic balancing act.

Finally, the combined effect of collaborative cultures serves to mobilize three powerful change forces. Moral purpose (the spiritual) gains ascendancy. Power (politics) is used to maximize pressure and support for positive action. Ideas and best practices (the intellectual) are continually being generated, tested and selectively retained. In collaborative cultures these three forces feed on each other. They become fused (chapter 6).

In the successful Chicago schools, for example, local participation expanded the moral authority, political will and access to ideas of school and community members: 'At base here is the moral force of a social movement,' say Bryk *et al.* (1998a, p. 254). Social cohesion is both a means and an end for achieving greater equity. It provides the socio-psychological strength for attacking different problems and for getting through rough times.

People, according to Brown and Eisenhardt (1998, p. 97), are the DNA of the process. They form the critical mass required for continuous development. But this is a superficial statement. So is all the lip service given to collegiality, collaboration and the professional learning community. Unless one understands deeply why and how collaboration functions to make a difference it is of little use. Once we do understand it better, we find out two things. One, it has surprising features — a lot more complexity, conflict and excitement than we might have imagined. Two, we find that there are profound conceptual bases from a number of different theoretical sources that converge to give us a great deal more confidence in the explanations for what is happening. We should consequently become more confident and certain that the risks involved in attempting to create collaborative structures and cultures are bound to be worth it. As Goleman (1998, p. 28) concludes: 'As work becomes more complex and collaborative, companies where people work together best have a competitive edge.' At the most fundamental level, could it be that we are witnessing a profound evolutionary reason for being optimistic? Could it be that, at the end of the day, cooperative groups thrive over selfish ones — that, with help, collaborative organizations and societies will eventually carry the day (Ridley, 1996, p. 175)? If so, the concept of collaboration must extend to the outside, a topic to which I now turn.

Chapter 4

The Deep Meaning of Outside Collaboration

To cope with a changing world, any entity must develop the capability of shifting and changing — of developing new skills and attitudes: in short, the capability of learning.

(De Gues, 1997, p. 20)

Internal ingenuity does not suffice when the environment is swirling. In this chapter, I will first view the outside from the perspective of the school. Then, I will shift to two outside-in perspectives, taking first the view of local authorities and second the vantage point of state-level authorities. The end result will be a deeper explanation of the necessity and meaning of outside collaboration. Put another way, the two-way street of 'inside-outside' is a far more powerful metaphor than top-down–bottom-up thinking.

Inside-Out

If there is anything that is underdeveloped in educational reform, it is the operational knowledge base that should be possessed and continually updated and refined by organizational members. Leonard (1995) confirms that effective organizations couple their internal problem-solving capacities with constant access to and consideration of external knowledge. She identifies other firms, universities, vendors, national labs, customers and consultants as sources of new technological knowledge. Productive organizations 'import and absorb knowledge from outside the firm.' Leonard found that companies with high absorptive capacity do six things. They:

1 create porous boundaries;
2 scan broadly;
3 provide for continuous interaction;
4 nurture technological gatekeepers;

5 nurture boundary spanners;
6 fight not-invented-here.

In 'creating porous boundaries', managers 'expose their companies to a bombardment of new ideas from outside in order to challenge core rigidities . . . if a company has antennae out into the world community and encourages employees to collect and disseminate that information internally, that knowledge is a treasure trove' (Leonard, 1995, pp. 155–6).

Second, these companies 'scan broadly': because knowledge comes from a diverse set of sources they cast the net widely (p. 156). The appetite for potential new breakthroughs is insatiable. Such companies are always tracking down new ideas that might be of benefit. They are involved in networks that make it inevitable that they will become aware of the latest ideas, and they vigorously check out promising new developments.

Another characteristic of companies skillful in importing knowledge is that they 'provide for continuous interaction', especially during new project development. Leonard cites Allen's study of low and high performing teams. Low performing teams either sought little information, or obtained it in lumps, while 'high performers kept up a consistent, continuous relationship with information sources of all types during the project' (p. 157).

Fourth and fifth, externally oriented companies 'nurture technological gatekeepers' (valuing and facilitating, for example, 'outstanding technical performers who keep their colleagues apprised of the latest happenings in the field' (p. 157)); they also hire 'boundary spanners' (especially in alliances and partnerships where knowledge utilization depends on understanding the cultures and knowledge of both partners).

Finally, absorptive capacity is negatively affected by the 'not-invented-here' syndrome (NIH): 'The term covers a multitude of common reactions, from a general distaste for adopting someone else's idea to . . . a (possibly correct) conviction that the new [idea] is flawed' (Leonard, 1995, p. 159). Leonard concludes:

> The most successful antidote to NIH is an organizational culture that embodies a sense of urgency for innovation, encourages interactions with outside sources of expertise, and helps employees understand the wellsprings of creativity — which are almost never filled in isolation. (p. 160)

Thus, close and regular contact with the environment is an essential condition for keeping up with the field. The reason that effective contact cannot be episodic is twofold: (a) too much is missed in a rapidly changing context, and (b) ongoing relationships are necessary in order to get at the deeper, tacit knowledge held by others. The latter aspect is one reason why networks and partnerships work; they provide a mechanism for accessing and converting the tacit knowledge of others into usable forms. In the words of Nonaka and Takeuchi (1995, p. 234):

> Creating knowledge is not simply a matter of processing objective information about customers, suppliers, competitors . . . the regional community or the government. [Organizational] members also have to mobilize the tacit knowledge held by these outside stakeholders through social interactions. Tapping the mental maps of customers is a typical example of this activity.

Most schools, it hardly needs saying, are not in the habit of seeking outside connections. A combination of norms and structures of privatism, rigid hierarchical bureaucracies, and in recent times, relentless attacks from the outside have kept most schools withdrawn from their environments. We have argued in our *What's Worth Fighting For Out There?* that this position is no longer tenable (or desirable). The 'out there' is now in here, in your face. Furthermore, it is an essential aspect of achieving success (Hargreaves and Fullan, 1998). The time for keeping the outside world at bay has passed.

Since the 'out there' is going to get you anyway, and since if you withdraw it will get you on its own terms, we concluded that 'the best way to deal with what's "out there" is 'to move toward the danger' (Hargreaves and Fullan, 1998, p. 67). In this argument, schools *need* the outside to get the job done. The ideas are out there as I have just argued; so are the partnerships required to mobilize technical and political forces for reform. Aspects of the outside environment can, of course, be hostile. All the more reason to enter the fray. Collaborative schools, like all interactive organizations, learn to make their way in difficult terrain. In fact, *because* they are collaborative internally, they are actually better at their work, know more, can explain themselves better and consequently have greater confidence in dealing with the outside.

The research on internally collaborative schools consistently shows that these schools engage the outside in their quest for continuous improvement. They do this in at least two ways: one involves political and moral mobilization; the other pertains to better knowledge and program creation.

We have already seen, for example, that Chicago schools pursuing systemic change vs. those who were only marginally involved in improvement were characterized by developing 'the engagement of parents and community resources':

> Schools pursuing a systemic agenda have a 'client orientation'. They maintain a sustained focus on strengthening the involvement of parents with the school and their children's schooling. They also actively seek to strengthen the ties with the local community and especially those resources that bear on the caring of children. As these personal interactions expand and become institutionalized in the life of the school, the quality of the relationships between local professionals and their community changes. Greater trust and mutual engagement begins to characterize these encounters. In contrast, schools with unfocused initiatives may set more distinct boundaries between themselves and their neighborhoods. Extant problems in these relationships may not be directly addressed. The broader community resources that could assist improvement efforts in the school are not tapped. These schools remain more isolated from their students' parents and their communities. (Bryk *et al.*, 1998a, pp. 127–8)

On the idea and knowledge side, these same schools habitually sought 'access to new ideas':

> For schools to restructure and renorm, a process of organizational learning must occur. New ideas must enter the school about core matters such as curriculum, instruction, and school organization. This introduction of proposed innovations often comes through personal connections of school staff to local colleges, universities, or other educational enterprises. It may be a natural consequence as new faculty are hired and bring with them new ideas to the school. In most general terms, the restructuring school is open to its external environment, actively seeking out and trying new ideas about how it might work differently. In contrast, schools with unfocused initiatives are more passive in this regard. They are less likely to actively seek out new information and more likely to just draw on whatever happens to cross their paths. Faculties in these schools remain more isolated and tend to repeat traditional practices. (Bryk *et al.*, 1998a, p. 128)

These actively restructuring schools in Chicago 'drew upon an extensive array of outside connections — including individual faculty at local colleges and universities, programs supported by area foundations, the business community, and other institutions — to guide and support their organizational development' (Bryk *et al.*, 1998a, p. 242).

Similarly, in Newmann and Wehlage's (1995) study of successful schools internal collaboration extended to encompass external use of staff development opportunities and external accountability standards. In cases where schools were immersed in continuous and coordinated staff development, 'the impact was schoolwide and much more powerful' (p. 43). Similarly, schools on the move made greater use of external standards (such as standards of performance in mathematics developed by state or national entities) in which 'staff were motivated to search for help and to draw ideas and insights from external resources about standards and how to put them into practice' (p. 43).

Successful organizations employ many methods of examining evaluation data about their performance. Most schools do not engage in reflective evaluation. But when assisted in developing this capacity, schools learn to take primary responsibility for their own improvement (Earl and Lee, 1998). The more the school collaborates and the more interesting changes it makes, the more that school staff seek (not avoid) evaluation data, including information generated through external standards assessment. Such schools actively seek external standards to test and extend their performance. They are data-driven by choice.

A Final Note on Inside-Out

While the above developments involving collaborative schools are exciting and are on the right track, they hardly represent the kind of creative living on the edge of chaos described by Stacey (1996), Brown and Eisenhardt (1998), Leonard (1995), Nonaka and Takeuchi (1995) and others. Schools, as I noted at the beginning of chapter 3, face many more constraints than entrepreneurial firms in their attempts to engage in innovative behavior. Even among the best schools we have no evidence that sustained knowledge creation is a feature of their work. Bryk *et al.* (1998a, p. 185) observe that in the most active schools 'efforts to promote more challenging intellectual work were still in their early stages', and that more attention had to be paid 'to enhancing the subject-matter knowledge and pedagogic expertise of individual teachers, and to developing as professional communities of practice' (p. 273).

There has been an explosion of knowledge and breakthroughs recently in the science of learning — brain research, cognitive science, the role of emotions, technology and more. We are still at the beginning of an intellectual burgeoning of the quality and depth of pedagogical knowledge and means of enhancing learning for all. This revolution has barely touched schools. The exciting part is that collaborative schools have entered the race, and in so doing are unleashing unprecedented change forces. Even the best inside-out schools are at the very early stages of this learning journey.

Outside-In: Local Districts

As we consider outside-in possibilities, there are two levels involved — one is extremely difficult; the other exceedingly difficult. These levels respectively are the local district or region, and the state level.

Local Education Authorities

Until very recently there were few if any detailed studies of the role of local school districts or agencies in managing change. The vast majority of research had focused on individual schools, not sets of schools operating within the same authority. Two excellent exceptions are the sophisticated studies of District #2 in New York City (Elmore and Burney, 1998) and of the Chicago Public School System (Bryk *et al.*, 1998a).

District #2 New York City

Elmore and Burney's (1998) study of District #2 in New York City is deeply insightful. District #2 contains forty-eight schools and is one of thirty-two districts in New York City. For a decade, through its superintendent, District #2 has pursued a strategy of system-wide instructional improvement. Elmore and Burney identify the seven 'organizing principles' of the strategy:

1. It's about instruction and only instruction;
2. Instructional improvement is a long, multistage process involving awareness, planning, implementation and reflection;
3. Shared expertise is the driver of instructional change;
4. The focus is on system-wide improvement;
5. Good ideas come from talented people working together;
6. Set clear expectations, then decentralize;
7. Collegiality, caring and respect. (pp. 4–5)

Using language reminiscent of Brown and Eisenhardt (1998) — 'improvisation and opportunism' in relation to some driving concepts — Elmore and Burney (1998) found five emerging themes:

1. Phased introduction of instructional changes organized mainly around content areas;
2. The intentional blurring between management of the system and the activities of staff development;
3. A complex and evolving balance between central authority and school site authority;
4. Unapologetic exercise of control in areas that are central to the decentralized strategy, most notably the recruitment, selection, training, and retention of staff;
5. Consistency of focus over time. (pp. 7–8)

Detailed strategies of instructional improvement in District #2 rely heavily on a coordinated but flexible staff development of all staff through: a professional development laboratory (where teachers spend three weeks of intensive observation and supervised practice in learning new ideas), instructional consulting services, intervisitations and peer networks, off-site training, and school site visits (district staff spend two days a week in schools reviewing plans and assessment data, visiting classrooms, discussing future steps with principals).

The district is data-driven but this is coupled with the kinds of sophisticated strategies identified throughout this book — a balance between too much and too little structure, lots of focused interaction and capacity-building of people and groups, and recognition of the uniqueness of each site. One result is that the aggregate data on reading and mathematics 'have shown steady gains from the inception of the district's improvement strategy' (Elmore and Burney, 1998, p. 12).

Elmore and Burney then move into a more fine-grained analysis of variability across schools, which reveals some of the more tacit theories, strategies and degrees of uniqueness that must be addressed school by school. This analysis provides detailed insights congruent with complexity theory and the lessons of change described in previous chapters. Thus, Elmore and Burney formulate five 'theory of action' principles that seemed to guide system-level administrators as they contended with the tension between system expectations and school variability:

Principle 1:   Principals are the key actors in instructional improvement.

Principle 2:   Each school presents a unique bundle of attributes into a unique set of instructional improvement problems: 'Systemic improvement required a high level of knowledge about the particularities of schools, but [district administrators] viewed this knowledge as critical intelligence about how to develop the competency of principals to deal with their settings and how to adapt district-level resources to the unique bundle of attributes and problems in the school' (p. 17).

Principle 3: Sustained instructional improvement is a process of bilateral negotiation between system-level administrators and principals: 'In all cases, there is no question that both system administrators and principals expect to negotiate, and the process of negotiation is the main vehicle by which they arrive at a common understanding of what will happen around instructional improvement in the school . . . In essence . . . bilateral negotiation is an arena for learning' (p. 18).

Principle 4: Common work among principals and teachers across schools is a source of powerful norms about system-wide instructional improvement: 'Professional development . . . takes the forms of activities designed to break down the isolation of principals and teachers' (p. 18).

Principle 5: Instructional improvement is primarily about the depth and quality of student work: 'As the strategy has matured . . . district administrators, and consequently professional developers and principals, have focussed increasingly on what they call high quality student work . . . [they seek] evidence of the increasing sophistication and complexity of student work' (p. 19).

This is no 'Christmas tree' district. *Ad hoc* projects and random professional development are seen as enemies of improvement. Schools are treated differently according to their circumstances, but student performance standards, best instructional practices and the development of a common culture are used as integrators. Elmore and Burney (1998, p. 29) found that 'principals perceive that they participate in a vertically integrated structure of values and learning opportunities that are designed to create a common culture.'

After ten years of development, the question is whether the work can be sustained 'as the strategy gets more complex' (Elmore and Burney, 1998, p. 35). Among the issues are: is the culture sufficiently developed and internalized to survive the departure of the superintendent (who has just taken a new position as chief academic officer in San Diego)? (The answer seems to be that the culture is indeed widely valued and internalized among leaders at school and district levels.) More telling is whether the district can go further, i.e. now that more complex student performance is being worked on, can the district engage in the kind of edge-of-chaos activities that will support and sustain the knowledge creation process required to achieve deep learning for students. As I have said, schools have not yet nearly evolved to the point where scientific breakthroughs in learning drive their interests.

Equally intriguing will be to watch the future of San Diego. The San Diego district is much larger and more complex (151 schools) and has already been working on developing a stronger infrastructure for systematic school improvement (Fullan and Watson, 1998). We can expect San Diego to work on making instructional improvement the main integrating strategy. Traditionally, school districts in North America have made professional development a staff function usually operating out of a separate non-line authority unit. In the new developments, line superintendents redefine their roles and responsibilities to focus primarily on instructional improvement strategies. In large districts this means dismantling independent staff development departments, and incorporating these responsibilities in area superintendents (responsible for families or clusters of schools). Thus, ongoing professional development becomes a major line responsibility of district administrators. Knowledge creation has to be the main business of learning organizations, and this is what developing districts must do.

Chicago School System

We have already seen the Chicago schools (as individual schools) in operation. Here I take a system perspective considering the 550 schools as a total set. The Chicago School System in fact is a good example of the 'too much–too little structure' dilemma identified earlier. According to Brown and Eisenhardt (1998) too much structure produces a rule-following culture, rigid processes and highly channeled communication. The result is 'loss of flexibility, stunted innovation, wrong products' (Brown and Eisenhardt, 1998, p. 42). Too little structure promotes rule-breaking, loose relationships and random communication producing confusion and unrealized products or services (p. 36).

Prior to 1988 when decentralization was legislated, Chicago was the embodiment of excessive bureaucracy that literally had ground the system to a halt. Too much structure took the form of an uncoordinated 'congery of bureaucracies [which] produced a maze of extra-school layers' (Bryk *et al.*, 1998a, p. 277). Overnight, in 1988 the system was decentralized with individual school authority handed over to 550 local school councils. From 1988 to 1994 the system operated in the decentralized fashion with little functional contact between schools and the district. In other words, too little structure characterized the operation. The result in the first instance (1988–94) was what Bryk *et al.* (1998a, p. 261) call the story of 'three-thirds'. One-third of the schools engaged in 'self-initiated active restructuring', one-third 'struggled with improvement' and one-third of the schools were 'left behind'. Even the self-initiating schools did not go very deep in instructional improvement. The district office, while much less influential, was still a negative factor: 'Four years into reform the basic orientation of the central office remained focussed on program compliance and emphasized control of local school practice' (Bryk *et al.*, 1998a, p. 278).

Since 1994 the central district was reorganized and restructured as a key player. It is still too early to assess its impact, but the gist of the change was to retain decentralized development within a context of capacity-building and external accountability — an attempt, in other words, to strike a balance between too much and too little structure. Two of the external researchers who have been tracking the reform (Bryk and Easton) had the opportunity to work full time in the district office during this reorganization. Their projective account of 'a new vision of central action' is thus particularly instructive, albeit partly speculative.

Bryk *et al.* (1998a, p. 279) argue that decentralization 'entails a renorming toward becoming advocates for local schools rather than acting as their superpatrons'; they refer to the need for new capacity-building external to the school, namely the establishment of 'the *extra-school infrastructure* needed to promote improvement' (p. 279, their italics).

Essentially, Bryk *et al.* advocate (entirely consistent with the cumulative analysis in this book) that four critical extra school functions must be developed:

1. Policy Making to Support Decentralization;
2. A Focus on Local Capacity Building;
3. A Commitment to Rigorous Accountability;
4. Stimulating Innovation. (Bryk *et al.*, 1998a, pp. 279–81)

First, policies, and goals and procedures need to be developed to support school development in the context of system expectations (much as we have just seen in District #2.)

Second, there is a 'need for significant advances in the knowledge, skill and dispositions of local school professionals, in their ability to work cooperatively together toward a more coherent school practice, and in their ability to effectively engage parents and the local community' (p. 280).

Third, a system of rigorous external accountability must be established 'that tracks the progress of schools' improvement efforts and that can intervene in failing situations' (p. 280). Further, 'it is central . . . that this accountability operate in ways that advance, rather than undermine local capacity-building.' Thus:

> Decentralization is based on the premise that the best accountability is not regulatory. While it may be necessary from time to time to use bureaucratic intervention in very troubled schools, the ultimate aim is a stronger base of professional norms of practice for educating all children well, coupled with supportive parent and community involvement toward the same ends. (p. 280)

Fourth, 'even though a decentralized system of schools no longer mandates programs for every school to implement, it still maintains a strong interest in spawning innovations and diffusing effective improvement efforts' (p. 281).

Finally, Bryk *et al.* (1998a) talk about the importance of distinguishing between some forms of external assistance which could come from intermediate providers like universities, profit and non-profit groups, learning networks and the like, and the kind of relationships that would exist with district offices including external accountability requirements.

The kinds of outside-in system transformation required for infrastructures of pressure and support to operate effectively, as I said at the outset, is an extremely difficult problem to address. Not only are there old structures and habits to break, but the new model itself is highly sophisticated in balancing top-down/bottom-up dilemmas.

On the positive side, the new model is deeply conceptually congruent with the complexity and evolutionary theories upon which this book is based. And it has growing empirical support as we have seen in the District #2 and Chicago cases. There is also support in our work with the Durham School Board in Ontario — a district with 114 schools — which progressed from a somewhat stagnant system in 1988 to being awarded the Bertelsmann prize in 1996 for being an outstanding innovative school system (Bertelsmann, 1996). Similarly, the Manitoba School Improvement Program in Winnipeg provides confirmation of the vital role of external assistance for local capacity-building. Earl and Lee (1998) describe the external role of pressure and support consisting of assistance with planning and problem-solving, support for evaluation, networking, professional development and expectations for accountability — all these as catalysts for the urgency–agency–energy engagement of teachers that they found in successful schools.

Despite these encouraging theoretical and empirical developments, I reiterate that these are very early versions of what will be needed to remake school systems into creative entities. Even the most advanced systems appear to be near the beginning of the evolutionary chain of complex adaptive organizations.

Finally, I would be amiss in not commenting on the superintendency in the United States. As long as volatility and faddism is practiced by local districts as they swing through superintendency after superintendency, it is impossible to establish the outside-in rapport that is required for sustained development. At the very least, one superintendency should build on the previous one. We now know what it takes to get a district on the right track. It takes an intensive effort over several years. All levels — schools and communities/districts (and states) — can conspire to focus on school development in the context of external accountability. There is something for both the left and the right to find in the most effective strategies for reform. Indeed, school districts who are making the most progress have superintendents whose tenure lasts six or more years. Another evolutionary point — the more we collaborate the greater the stabilization of the superintendency and, for that matter, the greater the stabilization of all leadership roles from principals to union leaders.

Outside-In: The State

Coordinating districts or regions is bad enough, but what about whole states, provinces or countries? Micklethwait and Wooldridge (1996, p. 294) remind us of two problems that plague public policymaking:

> The first is that the state is an incredibly blunt instrument; it gets hold of one overarching idea and imposes it without any sensitivity to the local context. The second is the desperate craving of politicians for a magical solution. (p. 121)

The consequences of these political vulnerabilities of large systems are *unrealistic timelines and policy clutter*. Policies are introduced without attention paid to the timelines and strategies of implementation that would be needed for success. The impatient search to address urgent problems makes the system susceptible to 'magical' (superficial) solutions. At the same time there are many urgent problems and frequent changes in government. So solutions get piled upon solutions creating overload and clutter. Even within the same government a new policy is introduced on top of yet-to-be implemented previous policies. The overall effect is constantly unfinished business in a context of fragmentation and incoherence.

Many governments, especially these days, make matters worse by focusing mainly on structural reform. Structures can be important, but not if they not only neglect but actually undermine capacity (the motivation, skills and resources) to concentrate on improvements in teaching and learning. Wallace and Pocklington (1998), for example, examine what happened when a structural policy to merge schools (due to under-utilization of space) was introduced in England. They talked about four features, only one of which helped implementation: 'policy vacuum' (no provision for how to implement the policy), 'policy insensitivity' (placing constraints on local action that turn out to be counterproductive), 'policy congruence' (incentives that do coincide with local needs) and 'policy contradiction' (when one policy is inconsistent with another). Similarly, in Ontario, Canada, the introduction of Bill 160 and related provisions to restructure school districts and their funding has created a massive diversion away from teaching and learning (see the special issue of *Orbit*, 1998). Clearly, at the local school and district levels (the previous section) these external structural interventions add insult to injury because they create enormous confusion and divert energies away from school improvement.

But what is a good government to do? If we take a long-term evolutionary perspective, the standard should be that governments over time increase their ability to produce 'healthy' societies akin to Wilkinson's analysis we saw in chapter 1: greater equality is achieved by investing in and monitoring capacity building, which produces greater social cohesion, which in turn generates greater health and wealth for the nation. It is not to deny the enormous inhibiting capacity of the prevailing power structure which favors the status quo to say that the long-run evolutionary question is whether the world can indeed achieve both greater equality and greater production of wealth.

No one has yet solved the problem of what the government's educational reform policies and strategies should be, largely because it is an incredibly complex challenge. Talk about chaos theory and complex adaptive systems! What could these policies and strategies possibly look like at the macro level? And is it remotely likely that they could evolve? We don't know the answers to these questions but the way to think about them and the lines of action are becoming clearer. What I have to say below is not a blueprint, but an agenda for action, development and future refinement. It is, if you like, an experiment in learning how to achieve large-scale reform.

I find Bryk *et al.*'s (1998a) framework for establishing local 'extra school infrastructures' to be entirely compatible with what needs to happen at the state or national level. It will be recalled that he and his colleagues identified four critical components of a new infrastructure (policymaking to support decentralization, local capacity-building, rigorous accountability and stimulating innovation): four components in combination and in interaction that would be required to make the infrastructure work.

First, a major review and overhaul of the *policy system* is required to ensure that it is supporting and pressing decentralization to the local district and school levels. Healey and De Stefano (1997) arrive at the same conclusion in their analysis of how to scale up school reform. As they say, the expansion and proliferation of good educational practice is obstructed by a plethora of obstacles: knowledge gaps, union contracts, lack of capacity, rules and regulations, interest groups, etc., (and, I would add, cluttered, misdirected government policies themselves). The idea, according to Healey and De Stefano (1997, p. 14) is to engage in *space-clearing* and *space-filling* policy development. This is not a legislative exercise but a series of activities and policy dialogue leading to changes in the legal structure of a system that could more clearly and better support local development. A good current example at the policy level is the follow-up work of the *National Commission on Teaching and America's Future* (NCTAF, 1996). Twelve states signed on:

> Each partner state agreed to assemble a broad-based policy group that would ensure the involvement of key stakeholders, including representatives from the governor's office; relevant state education agencies; boards having authority for teacher education as well as elementary, secondary, and higher education; professional associations; state legislators; leaders from the business community; and other public education and community advocates. Each state's policy group is responsible for receiving the results of a policy inventory that examines the full range of teacher-related issues — recruitment, preparation, licensing, induction, certification, and ongoing professional development — as well as the broader issues of student standards and reform. (Darling-Hammond, 1997, p. 6)

In effect, the first requirement says 'trust policies that focus on decentralization'. The remaining three elements say 'don't trust them completely', that is, don't leave effective decentralization up to chance.

The second requirement, then, is to *invest in local capacity-building*. Healey and De Stefano (1997) observe that reform is successful when there is significant demand for it at the local level, widespread involvement and skills and dispositions to engage in reform activities. These things cannot be mandated, but investing in intermediate agencies and corresponding activities can stimulate their development. What is involved is directly and indirectly providing opportunities for advancing the knowledge, skills and work of local school and district personnel along the lines of what we know about creating powerful learning communities (chapter 3). Another example is the development of a range of capacity-building activities designed to support parents and others in pre-school education and development — a capacity that pays off manifold as children enter school.

Third, a *rigorous accountability system* is essential. This is both a policy and a capacity-building proposition. We have already seen that a framework of external standards for student performance is an essential ingredient for reform at the school level. This system should generate and make available data on student achievement, but it also must be done with an *explicit philosophy of decentralization* underpinning its efforts. The first goal of external accountability, say Bryk *et al.* (1998a, p. 291), is to shape the terms of discussion among professionals and parents at the school and district levels in terms of 'what educational goals for children are worth holding; what quality instruction looks like; and how overall school operations might be structured to create environments more conducive for student learning.' In short, 'productive central strategy turns first to an educative tool, rather than direct regulation, to influence local action' (p. 291). At the same time, an additional aim of external accountability is the 'identification of non-improving schools': 'When school [or district] initiative is not undertaken and external assistance fails, consequences must ensue' (Bryk *et al.*, 1998, p. 292). As long as governments sincerely believe in and invest in decentralization (and everything I have said in this book confirms that this is essential), there is room for intervention in persistently non-performing schools and districts.

The establishment of such a sophisticated accountability system (technically and philosophically) is no easy task. The agencies responsible for generating and conducting accountability reviews should be at least quasi-independent of the government in order to preserve the integrity of the system, as Bryk *et al.* (1998a, p. 303) recommend and as is the case in Ontario with the recently established Education Quality and Accountability Office. In addition to the availability of good data, the *process* of quality reviews must engage schools and districts in examining what they are doing and in developing corresponding actions (this is the educative and capacity-building function). At the same time, this does not mean that the quasi-independent agency is responsible for acting on the results. Support for further development, and intervention in cases of continued low performance is the responsibility of authority agencies whether they be local or state level. All of this will take some doing because the technology of assessment is complex, as is the balancing act required of a system that is simultaneously educative and evaluative.

In summary, one key role of the external accountability system is to help build local capacity for examining and taking action on assessment data — what we have called 'assessment literacy' (Hargreaves and Fullan, 1998). The other role is to intervene in persistently failing schools and school systems. Combining these educative and evaluative roles requires great sophistication and judgment.

Fourth, since new ideas are crucial, and since the education system is traditionally weak at accepting and spreading new knowledge and practices, a deliberate *system of stimulating innovation* is required. This involves enlivening the marketplace of ideas and providing access to them. To a large extent the marketplace is already well on its way. Governments, foundations and other profit and non-profit agencies are all currently engaged in helping to produce new ideas and practices and making them available. Governments need to review their own portfolios to determine what needs to be done to stimulate the market further, and above all what can be done to make it easier for people to learn about ideas developed elsewhere. The innovative infrastructure is crucial because ideas and knowledge are proliferating at an astounding rate around the world. Chapter 4 makes the case for establishing strong two-way connections between schools and the outside in order to access ideas on a continuous base, while chapter 3 claims that the conditions for quality implementation must be built within schools.

States and nations have not yet explicitly put their minds to establishing 'reform infrastructures' of the nature and scope we are talking about here. An interesting new example is *The Implementation of The National Literacy Strategy* (Department for Education and Employment, 1997) and the corresponding 'National Numeracy Strategy' in Britain. The Literacy Strategy states that 'by the year 2002, 80% of all 11 year-olds will reach the standard expected for their age' (DfEE, 1997, p. 5). This goal by itself is not noteworthy, since many governments have set ambitious targets for the future. What is different is that the goals are backed up with comprehensive implementation strategies that include: initial teacher education, professional development, local plans, assessment and feedback, family programs, national activities and the like. This is the most ambitious implementation strategy undertaken by a major government. It will be interesting to track the experience and impact of this unique national initiative because of its explicit commitment to building in reform infrastructures at many levels.

The role of the state outlined above presents fantastic challenges. The farther one gets from the 'inside', the harder it is for the 'outside' to exercise control, and therein lies the key to reprioritizing government strategy. When it comes to large-scale reform, the more obvious direct strategy (here is a problem, and here is the solution) does not work. It cannot work because of complexity and evolutionary theories which confirm that systems change through more indirect (yet more powerful) learning and living mechanisms. Instead of attempting to first control and then educate, governments need to reverse the strategy. In the same way that Bryk *et al.* (1998a, p. 279) conclude that districts must become advocates for local schools rather than superpatrons, states must become advocates for local districts. *First educate then control.* By letting go and investing in the properties of complex adaptive systems, governments paradoxically cause more change in practice, which is where it counts.

The Deep Meaning of Outside Collaboration

Figure 4.1 summarizes the deep meaning of inside-out collaboration in terms of five characteristics. Whether one takes the school district or the local–state relationship, and whether one takes an inside-out or outside-in perspective, we end up with the same conclusion. The first deep meaning of outside collaboration is that it is not instrumental, it is symbiotic. To survive we need to learn from the environment and it (other people and organizations) needs to learn from us. The sooner we learn that it is a two-way street, the more we and the larger system will develop. Valuing reciprocity is of critical importance.

Second, in so learning we must constantly struggle with the balance of too much and too little structure. If we try to exercise control

Figure 4.1   Characteristics of inside-out collaboration for complex times

- Reciprocity — the two-way street
- Balancing too much/too little structure
- Deepening the intellectual
- Deepening the political
- Deepening the spiritual

(too much structure) over our environment, or if those outside try to control us, we will fail. If we try to ignore structure (too little) we will get destroyed. Engaging in diverse, continuous relationships with the outside, ranging from close working alliances to market-like explorations (again built-in, not episodic), is the second deep characteristic.

The first two features refer to orientations and mechanisms, while the next three provide the substance. Third, in turbulent, changing environments, continuous processing of new knowledge is fundamental to growth. Especially in education, where scientific breakthroughs are abounding and where new pedagogical solutions are badly needed, the intellectual strength of school systems can only be enhanced by paying close attention to the worldwide knowledge base. By connecting closely to diverse environments schools place themselves in a position to deepen their intellectual capacity on a continuous basis.

Moving forward requires the mobilization of moral commitment, not just passively espousing the right things. It involves overcoming scores of internal and external obstacles. Teaming up with forces in the environment to generate commitment, expectations and accountability is a political act. Deepening political commitment to a course of action is the fourth characteristic.

The more we work with wider and wider environments, the more likely we are to discover the profound spiritual meaning of what Senge (1990) called 'the indivisible whole': 'All boundaries, national boundaries included, are fundamentally arbitrary. We invent them and then, ironically, we find ourselves trapped within them' (Senge, 1990, p. 98). Not getting trapped in our own self-sealing world is the fifth deep meaning of external collaboration. By extending purposeful alliances to diverse outside partners we gain moral meaning in educational reform and contribute to its spread.

Finally, it is crucial to note that it is not just a matter of establishing the components of the external infrastructure as if it were a check list. What makes infrastructures work is the quality of conceptualization and the nature of the philosophy that underpins them. Those who are developing infrastructures must work hard at deepening their conceptualization of how the four components — decentralization policies, local capacity-building, accountability and innovation–stimulation — can feed on each other. At the same time, the conceptualization of infrastructure must be driven by a philosophy of moral purpose and human development in which capacity-building and accountability learn to work together.

Final Notes on Across-Boundary Collaboration

First, it is instructive to return to the role of anxiety. Stacey (1996b) observed that anxiety and creativity within organizations are related, provided that the organization has anxiety-containing strengths. The same relationship holds between organizations (schools) and educational (districts) and state (government) systems. By definition, high levels of anxiety will always exist in complex systems, and indeed discomfort is a condition of creative problem solving. The deepest meaning of inside-out/outside-in collaboration is keeping anxiety in balance, simultaneously provoking and containing it. This finding also shows why it is folly for governments only to provoke anxiety — they must also contribute to its containment through support.

Second, I treated parents and community as part of the inside-out equation. In ideal circumstances schools would establish a unity with their communities. In too many cases, however, parents and the community are actually outsiders. In fact, this appears to be the norm. Coleman (1998) found that collaboration with parents was not well developed, yet it was an alterable variable which schools and teachers can do something about. Says Coleman (1998, p. 43): 'The most important task facing the school in the immediate future is collaboration with parents in building active communities of learners.' When schools don't respond by reaching out to parents, communities must act and be helped to act. Policies and assistance supporting parent involvement are required to raise expectations and possibilities for schools to extend their boundaries (see Epstein, 1997, and Hargreaves and Fullan, 1998).

There is also a case to be made for directly focusing on community development as an independent force for reform. Regardless of social class, it is hard for good schools to evolve in bad communities, and it is hard for schools not to feel the pressure and support to be good if the community is developing. Both the school and the community can contribute to each other's development.

Third, the inside-out and outside-in discussion in this chapter tended to favor one-way influences in either direction. In fact, as we have seen in the first characteristic — reciprocity — our theory stresses mutual respect and mutual impact. The more that schools act in an inside-out collaborative mode, the more they will influence the world around them, locally and even nationally as their efforts form a consistent critical mass calling for a new way of working. Outside-in forces must also learn from as well as instruct local development. The more that district and state entities learn from local action — something that they are not used to doing — the greater the chances for widespread change.

Two-way inside-outside reciprocity is the elusive key to large-scale reform. There are no one-sided shortcuts to the transferability and dissemination of educational reform. The intractability of scaled-up reform is one of the most perplexing and illustrative instances of complexity theory in action. Chapter 5 reveals why transferability runs into so many problems.

The Complexities of Transferability

[We] can tour competitors through the plant, show them almost every-
thing and we will be giving away nothing because they can't take it
home with them.

(CEO of Chaparral, cited in Leonard, 1995, p. 7)

You should never worry about your good ideas being stolen in educational reform, because even when people are sincerely motivated to
learn from you, they have a devil of a time doing so. Transferability of
ideas is a complex problem of the highest order.

The Difficulties of Transferability

There are at least three interrelated reasons why innovations are difficult to disseminate and replicate. The first is that the *products* of other
people's reform efforts hide many of the subtleties of the reform in
practice. Schorr (1997) states:

> What is essential is invisible to the eye. The practitioners know more
> than they can say. In the words of MIT Professor Don Schön, they
> operate with an 'Iceberg of tacit knowledge and artistry beneath the
> surface of readily accessible descriptions' of effective practices. (p. 29)

Leonard (1995) makes the same point about importing technological
knowledge:

> Market scarce skills may be firm specific and based in the experience
> of longtime employees. These characteristics make such skills difficult
> to transfer . . . the tacit knowledge of people even quite far down the
> organizational ladder, and not explicitly recognized as experts, may
> be an essential part of the technological capability being acquired.
> (p. 165)

Moreover, there may be a difference between espoused values or
general values stated in descriptions of a reform, and enacted values

practiced on a day-to-day basis: 'These kinds of little values that determine the screening and rewarding of different types of knowledge tend to be implicit' (Leonard, 1995, p. 167). Reading detailed descriptions, observing videos and even site visits do not capture enough of the reality of the innovation in action. And when there is open sharing, practitioners often 'know more than they can say' so this too is insufficient.

This problem of product transfer is compounded by the search for magical solutions and other shortcuts. It *would* be great if someone else had the answer and we could take it on. This vulnerability leads to the 'Christmas tree' schools I referred to earlier — indiscriminately adding innovation after innovation (Bryk *et al.*, 1998a). The trap is that 'ideas acquired with ease are discarded with ease' (Pascale, 1990, p. 20). In short, there is really no such thing as easy product transfer in social reform. Innovation is not a pill, a widget or a silver bullet.

The second and deeper reason that transferability is complex is that successful reforms in one place are partly a function of good ideas, and largely a function of the *conditions* under which the ideas flourished. Successful innovations, argue Healey and De Stefano (1997), fail to be replicated because the wrong thing is being replicated — the reform itself, instead of the conditions which spawned its success. Success stories are success stories because:

> (1) the reform addressed a well-understood local need, (2) there is a significant local demand for the reform, (3) the reform itself is locally derived, (4) it is championed by one or more 'messiahs', (5) it is adequately financed, and (6) there is widespread ownership of the reform. Attempting to replicate the reform itself (i.e., take it to scale) *inevitably* violates some of the very conditions that render certain innovations successful in the first place. The fact is that people's educational aspirations, needs and contexts differ from place to place. Accordingly, what works in one location won't necessarily work in another. And even in those instances where an 'outside' innovation addresses some of the specific needs and aspirations of a particular location, its fate is still precarious, for unless there is widespread ownership of the innovation (a factor largely engendered through the development of local solutions), chances are that it will not become a permanent part of that location's educational landscape. Instead of replication of the reform itself, we contend that it is the *conditions which give rise to the reform in the first place* that should be replicated. (Healey and De Stefano, 1997, pp. 10–11, italics in original)

It helps if the designers of innovations and those facilitating dissemination have developed a theory of action (e.g. a set of strategies for addressing local conditions) as well as a theory of education. Schorr (1997, p. 148) reports that of twenty-nine directors of youth development projects in the midwest, when 'asked about the theory behind their projects, only one responded with anything resembling a theory.' That is, these change facilitators had no conception or theory to guide their actions. A positive example, is the Child Development Project (CDP) which I reported on earlier (Lewis *et al.*, 1998). In further evaluation, Coburn and Meyer (1998) found that CDP succeeded because as a model it encompassed both a theory of pedagogical reform and a theory of shaping 'context' (i.e. local conditions). CDP is:

> a reform initiative distinctive both for its philosophical emphasis (simultaneously attending to the social, ethical and intellectual dimensions of learning) and its reform strategy fostering a supportive reform context by engaging multiple stakeholders in implementing and sustaining reform. (Coburn and Meyer, 1998, p. 2)

Even with strong external support designed to engage multiple levels of the system, CDP became well implemented in only about half of the sites (six of twelve schools in six districts, Lewis *et al.*, 1998). In a sub-study, Coburn and Meyer (1998) found school-wide implementation in four of the five schools in their sample. As part of the context, Coburn and Meyer (1998) emphasize how important it is to include the role of the district or local authority as part of the reform strategy. Evidence of strong involvement was found in two of the three districts which actively worked to sustain and spread CDP into the work of the district.

Most reform initiatives at best have a theory of education, and rarely have a theory of action to address local context or conditions. Let me stress how complex this problem is. Even with a well worked out theory of action, reform initiatives face incredible difficulties pertaining to tacit knowledge, local prehistory, local politics and personalities, and so on. But at least you are in the game if you have a theory of action which accompanies your other good ideas.

Third, deeper still (and here we come full circle) reform on a large scale depends on *the development of local capacity to manage multiple innovations simultaneously*. In other words, we are talking about fundamental transformation of institutions on a wide scale. To put it perversely, if many different reform initiatives developed well-honed theories of education and theories of action, and then independently attempted to engage schools, this would compound the problem of complexity. One way out is, of course, that a really well-honed theory of action by definition would take into account whatever multiple innovations local institutions faced. This shows how complex change theory is; it must take into account multiple priorities that continuously impinge on individuals and organization.

The development of local capacity, thousands of times over, is therefore the ultimate complex problem because *each* local situation to a certain extent will be unique and will need to develop differently depending on the particular configuration of its evolution. In this sense, it is not just addressing directly the six conditions identified by Healey and De Stefano (1997) earlier in this section. Returning to the 'living systems' metaphor, it is the dynamic movement of a complex set of interacting local conditions that must change. As we have seen throughout this book, there are ways of making the problem worse, and there are even ways of guiding the process, but it can't be controlled, which is the main reason why 'competing on the edge' is so difficult to imitate (Brown and Eisenhardt, 1998, p. 23).

A Way Ahead

We are at the very early stages of appreciating the nature and complexity of educational reform on a large scale. There have been attempts at large-scale reform earlier in the century, but they lacked the critical analysis we are now able to bring to bear on the problem. Elmore (1995) traces the problem after starting with the observation:

> A significant body of circumstantial evidence points to a deep, systemic incapacity of U.S. schools and the practitioners in them, to develop, incorporate, and extend new ideas and teaching and learning in anything but a small fraction of schools and classrooms. (p. 1)

Elmore, as others have concluded, says that the closer an innovation gets to the core of schooling, the less likely it will influence teaching and learning. In my terms this is because reculturing (which gets at the core of teaching and learning) is much more difficult than restructuring. Elmore analyses why the Progressive Period in the first half of the century failed to take hold. Among other things, progressive reformers made the mistake of turning inward — a good strategy for small-scale innovation but fatal for larger-scale impact.

> Rather than persist in Dewey's original agenda of influencing public discourse about the nature of education and its relation to society

through open public discussion, debate and inquiry, the more militant progressives become increasingly like true believers in a particular version of the faith and increasingly isolated from public scrutiny and discourse. In this way, the developers of progressive pedagogy become increasingly isolated from the public mainstream and increasingly vulnerable to attack from traditionalists. (Elmore, 1995, p. 11)

You could say that their theory of education in the absence of a theory of action drove them down a path of self-destruction.

Similarly, the large-scale curriculum development projects of the 1950s and 1960s came to naught. These strategies focused on ideas, conducted countless in-service workshops, but almost totally neglected the culture of the institutions which were to be the hosts of these innovations (Elmore, 1995; Fullan, 1991).

After the aborted attempts at large-scale reform in the 1960s, serious attempts at large-scale reform disappeared for almost two decades in the US. The growing dissatisfaction around the world with the performance of public schools and the associated belief that in knowledge societies surely 'education' must become an agent of societal development has catapulted the question of large-scale reform back to the top of the agenda. How can we approach the problem more productively this time? Figure 5.1 lists four interrelated ideas for moving ahead.

Figure 5.1   Ideas for moving ahead on large-scale reform

- Use complexity theory for achieving new freedom
- Transfer capabilities not products (invest in capacity building)
- Invest in the long term
- Combine (integrate) different theories, programs and people

First, use complexity theory. It should be abundantly clear that the notion that knowledge about change can be packaged and delivered is absurd. Just as we have concluded that students have to construct their own meaning for learning to occur, people in all local situations must also construct their own change meaning as they go about reform. Once we know this it can be quite liberating as we give up narrow prescriptive strategies in trying to get people to conform — strategies that we know through experience do not work. If there is any prescription, Stacey (1996b, p. 278) says it 'is to use the insights of complexity science as a framework for individual, group, and organization-wide self-reflection.' Stacey proceeds to argue:

People who begin to think differently will almost certainly begin to act differently, and they will then almost certainly affect someone else who will begin to behave differently. (1996b, p. 278)

Precise descriptions are 'an invitation for people to stop thinking' (p. 278). Storr (1997, p. 233) makes the same point about gurus: 'The charisma of certainty is a snare which entraps the child who is latent in us all.' Stacey (1996b) quotes the manager who talks about the impact of complexity theory on himself:

> As I have read about complexity theory I feel like I have become aware of a new world around me . . . I discovered ethnography and more importantly action learning and reflection-in-action . . . Almost straight away my behavior changed. I began openly asking people for their thoughts and assumptions behind statements when they came up in discussion and when I disagreed with them. Almost immediately I felt much more satisfied with my inputs and with the responses I was getting from people, particularly with the factory manager I am working with . . . We have a time set aside to reflect now — it kind of happens though — not in a planned way. This line of thinking opened the box though . . . Time after time we are exploring the motivation and potential assumptions behind behavior as we see it and attempting to modify ours to continue to develop support and momentum for change. (pp. 278–9)

Knowledge is about beliefs (commitment), meaning and action, which is why it must be developed not borrowed (Nonaka and Takeuchi, 1995, p. 58). Development in social settings is a complex act. Hence complexity theory provides us with the best orientation.

Second, we do not, however, have to wait around for people to discover complexity theory. Conceiving of transferability or large scaleness as the flow of *capabilities* rather than products opens up a whole new agenda of strategies. To know that large-scale reform is a function of social propagation is to know that the large-scale transfer of complex good ideas is almost impossible 'in the absence of intimate personal contact' (Nonaka and Takeuchi, 1995, p. 223). Investing in capacity-building means increasing the amount and variety of interaction:

> To nurture the highly subjective and personal mindset of individuals within the company, a knowledge-creating company should provide a place where a rich source of original experience can be gained — what we are calling a high-density field. A high-density field refers to an environment in which frequent and intensive interactions among crew members take place. (Nonaka and Takeuchi, 1995, p. 230)

We have already seen the 'deep meaning' of internally collaborative cultures (chapter 3) and of highly interactive networks to the outside (chapter 4). We also see why developing certain leadership capabilities is crucial. Middle-level managers, like principals, are in the best position to conduct a middle-up-down management way of working, which serves to integrate various sources of knowledge (Nonaka and Takeuchi, 1995, p. 232). And we have seen that investing in local capacity, far from reducing accountability, actually increases it. For one thing, external standards and associated information are one of the primary sources of deliberation and knowledge-creation in highly interactive organizations. For another thing, high-density interaction inside and outside the organization is one of the strongest, most organic built-in forms of accountability that any human system has yet to devise. Lateral accountability is always more effective than hierarchical accountability. Finally, the transfer of capabilities means those capabilities that meet the test of constant refinement and quality assurance — what Elmore (1995, p. 18) calls the development of 'strong external normative structures of practice'. Capacity-building includes the continual flow and integration of the best ideas available.

Third, because the development of capabilities takes time, it is essential that a mid- to long-term perspective be taken. So far this has not been politically attractive. Policymaking is a world of adoption of the latest would-be solutions. It is a world of putting new policies 'on the books' through legislation and other means. The timeline to the next election is always shorter than the timeline for capacity-building. Yet when organizations do invest in the long term (provided that they focus on the right things and make connections as they go along) they do eventually make a difference, and before too long. Durham school district went from a stagnant to a moving school system with its 114 schools in about eight years (Bertelsmann, 1996). District 2 in New York (48 schools) was transformed in less than ten years (Elmore and Burney, 1998). Most remarkable is Chicago in which a persistent, adjusted, sophisticated strategy evolved and made a significant difference in large numbers of the over 400 elementary schools (Bryk *et al.*, 1996a). There are several implications from these three examples: (a) it did take the better part of a decade in which it was not at all clear after a few years that success would be achieved; (b) all three districts practiced 'support and pressure' capacity-building strategies and obtained cumulative results because of these strategies; (c) they were reflective about the strategies using data and feedback to adjust or add components to address weaknesses or gaps as their experiences evolved; (d) none of these systems can be declared a once and for all success

— much more remains to be done and it is not at all clear that these systems can sustain their extraordinary efforts; (e) and these are only districts (albeit large), not large-scale systems like whole states.

For truly large-scale reform, the state itself must engage in capacity building of the kind we see in these three districts, and it must do so over a decade or more if we are to see widespread results. The aim, according to Healey and De Stefano (1998), is to establish an external reform structure in which states and their departments of education:

> redefine their roles away from the top-down, command-style, hyper-regulation, supply-mode approach that currently predominates in many education systems to one that is more open, outworldly accountable, and responsive; and that collaborates with clients in providing education services. In particular, we are interested in both the degree to which, and the manner in which, education departments at all levels acquire and apply skills regarding data analysis . . . and communication. (pp. 19–20)

So far there are no examples of this level of commitment and sophistication at the level of the state. The government that figures out how to do this, and in so doing enhances its chances of getting re-elected, will be the government of the future.

Fourth, I am not talking about promoting a flurry of discrete projects. School systems need integration, wholeness and at least periods of coherence. The paradox is that greater coherence in complex societies can only be achieved by grappling with differences and combining strategies and components that have hitherto been pursued independently from each other. Thus, for example, the strategy of going where the energy is or supporting groups of like-minded innovators is seriously flawed.

> This strategy immediately isolates the teachers who are most likely to change from those who are least likely to embrace reform. This dynamic creates a social barrier between the two, virtually guaranteeing that the former will not grow in number and the latter will continue to believe that exemplary teaching requires extraordinary resources in an exceptional environment. (Elmore, 1995, p. 17)

The pressure and support scenarios depicted by the lessons for change and collaboration in previous chapters create better conditions for reaching the critical mass of *diverse* participants which will be required for scaled-up reform.

At the same time, large-scale reform will require mobilizing and coordinating more components of the system. Current reform strategies, as Hill and Celio (1998) insightfully argue, serve to segment different initiatives resulting in fragmentation of effort. Hill and Celio identify seven different major strategies for reform currently being debated and promoted by some sectors of society:

- standards;
- teacher development;
- new school designs;
- decentralization and site-based management;
- charter schools;
- school contracting;
- vouchers.

Each of the strategies, the authors claim, have 'zones of wishful thinking', i.e. they assume that certain actions will be taken, but there is nothing in the intervention *per se* that would make this likely. For example, vouchers assume 'that entrepreneurs will offer good schools in poverty areas where teaching can be difficult and parents are less demanding' (Hill and Celio, 1998, pp. 1–7). Hill and Celio proceed to compile a list of events for each of the seven reform theories 'that the reform needs but cannot cause' (pp. 1–10). In my terms, these reform strategies contain elements of a theory of education but lack comprehensive theories of action needed to address related conditions, which would have to be altered in order for success to occur.

The bad news is that this is a really complex problem — how to combine and integrate the strengths of different reform strategies, many of which are perceived to be fundamentally different in approach, and each of which has advocates who are in competition. The good news, according to Hill and Celio (1998, pp. 1–10) is: 'A surprising discovery that emerged from our comparison of the cause and effect assumptions of different reform proposals was their potential complementarity.'

It is still a difficult problem, but we have a new and very promising line of thinking for integrating the strengths of different approaches and achieving more comprehensive, and thus more powerful, reform strategies.

Hill and Celio (1998, pp. 3–15) then present us with 'the strange co-existence of harsh disagreements about the way in which public education should change, with apparent agreement about the attributes of a good school and how school changes can lead to increased student learning.'

They label the points of agreement as 'integrative capital':

A school's integrative capital is a unifying vision that establishes:
- What ideas, facts, and habits the school intends to help students learn;
- What learning experiences the school intends to offer students and how the school intends to provide those experiences in order to ensure that students do learn;
- What students the school intends to serve (defined by age groups, prior education, and other characteristics);
- How the school will relate to those children's parents and the public officials responsible to act in the children's interests. (Hill and Celio, 1998, pp. 3–5)

Echoing ideas I have already discussed in chapters 3 and 4, Hill and Celio (1998, pp. 3–15) observe:

Integrative capital looks beneath the phenomenon of collaboration to the ideas about teaching and learning that underlay it. The concept of integrative capital, in short, sees leadership, shared commitment, and collaboration as results of something deeper, i.e., goals for students and a strategy of teaching and learning that can help students reach those goals.

Still, the problems are manifold. First, if you don't have high integrative capital, how do you get it? This is the theory of action in which there are no shortcuts because it means working on the edge of chaos, balancing between too much and too little structure. Second, how do you get different groups, who see themselves as having nothing in common and may see each other as enemies, to cooperate and draw on each other's strengths? As Hill and Celio (1998, p. 24) say:

Most public schools are now products of geological layers of regulations, half-implemented past reform initiatives, and bargains among adults. These structures promote isolation of parts of the school from one another, and their cumulative effect, when seen across a school, is fragmentation.

Third, what if it turns out that some of the purported commonalities evaporate when issues of reducing disparity between groups are really tackled. Equity is often a victim when small-scale successes attempt to go to scale (Oakes *et al.*, 1998).

On balance, however, given rampant fragmentation, given several areas of common agreement and given the crying need to go to scale, i.e. to transform the whole system, a whole new domain of reform strategies needs to be mined and developed. The new approaches at the system level are not completely clear because we are at the very early stages of rethinking a deeply complex problem, but the lines of action are becoming more evident. Hill and Celio's (1998) outline is remarkably congruent with the conclusions emerging in this book. They say:

- Separate immediate management from long-term planning;
- Look for the roots of the problem;
- Rely on an outside institution as a critical friend;
- Assemble diverse groups of experts to get beyond local politics;
- Seek help from the state;
- Redesign the system by focussing on developing schools with strong integrative capital. (Hill and Celio, 1998, ch. 5)

Whereas Bryk *et al.* (1998) called for strategies that incorporate 'accountability, assistance, and autonomy', Hill and Celio (1998) talk about the same concepts as 'incentives, capabilities, and opportunities'.

We can say that every system-wide reform strategy must create *incentives for school performance, ways of increasing school capabilities, and opportunities and freedoms for school staff to change how they serve students.* (Hill and Celio, 1998, pp. 5–12, italics in original)

There is, in other words, a growing consistency about what is needed, and it represents a sophisticated combination of strategies.

A Final Note

What is the relationship between transferability and going to scale? If we stick with single innovations, even major ones, a combination of good ideas/programs and a receptive/seeking institution is required for quality reforms to reach a large audience. In this respect, widespread transferability of a program *is* going to scale. Schorr (1997) confirms this conclusion when she states that successful social improvement programs have seven attributes:

1. Successful programs are comprehensive, flexible, responsive, and persevering.
2. Successful programs see children in the context of their families.
3. Successful programs deal with families as parts of neighborhoods.

4. Successful programs have a long-term preventive orientation, a clear mission, and continue to evolve over time.
5. Successful programs are well managed by competent and committed individuals with clearly identifiable skills.
6. Staff of successful programs are trained and supported to provide high-quality, responsive services.
7. Successful programs operate in settings that encourage practitioners to build strong relationships based on mutual trust and respect. (Schorr, 1997, pp. 5–12)

These conclusions, then, are valuable for any proponents of major, potentially effective program interventions.

If you look closely at another of Schorr's (1997) findings you can turn the basic conclusion on its head. One of her conclusions about past failures is that 'we failed to see that you can't grow roses in concrete' (p. 29). And, to ensure that the essence of a reform takes hold, 'you do that by not ignoring the institutional context, and by not leaving the responsibility for creating a more hospitable context to the front line people, who are not in a position to change the wider environment' (Schorr, 1997, p. 30).

To change the wider environment! Flipping the problem on its head, this means that you have to directly work on changing the context of recipient organizations, i.e. you need to develop local capacity for showing an interest in, deciding on and incorporating good ideas into practice. You need, in other words, to focus on the development of local capacity, the quality of external reform infrastructures and the relationship between the two. Ultimately, going to scale does not mean the spread of *ad hoc* proven programs; it means developing the capacity of the system (local capacity and external infrastructure in combination) to manage and integrate the complexity of innovations and choices that abound. Going to scale does not mean getting the latest program in place (although this can be valuable in a narrow, temporary sense), but rather it means developing the capacity of the multilevel system to manage complex change on a continuous basis.

This is indeed a tall order, but going to scale means fundamentally developing the system at all levels. Otherwise one cannot achieve, let alone sustain, large-scale reform. If you can't grow roses in concrete you need to change the concrete. Transferability leads us back to the deep meaning of collaboration inside and outside the school. 'Changing the concrete' is the agenda because that is the way that organizations will learn to seek ideas and make wise decisions on an ongoing basis about the array of ideas and programs that are available.

When all is said and done, the capacity for transferability in a social system is a function of the quality of the infrastructure. The more the infrastructure builds in continuous learning, generates accountability data, promotes feedback, stimulates innovation and so on, the more the system is capable of large-scale reform. In effect, strong infrastructures access tacit and explicit knowledge on a continuous basis and make it widely available.

The availability of knowledge by itself will not result in comprehensive reform. In complex systems, we cannot limit ourselves to the already knowable. We must work to establish the infrastructure which will enable us to create and seek new knowledge as we go, and we must pursue more ambitious system-level goals (such as increasing literacy for all students). Transferability and large-scale reform urges all of us to pay attention to the big picture. This is not the time for modest goals.

In short, going to scale equals system transformation! To accomplish this, individuals, groups, institutions and society will need to mobilize the major forces which are central to reform. They will, in a phrase, need to mobilize and fuse all the intellectual, political and spiritual forces they can muster.

Chapter 6

Intellectual, Political and Spiritual Fusion

*When fusion occurs it produces **five times** the energy. Fusion is about joining, coming together, creating connection.*
(Daft and Lengel, 1998, p. 15, emphasis in original)

This book is about the everlasting tension between diversity and reconciliation. Time and again we have seen that differences contain the seeds of creativity, but the route to reconciliation is complex and anxiety prone. Saul (1997, p. 299) talks about societal development in the following terms:

> [It] is a humanist movement seeking continual reform in order to improve the life of the community. This does include economic well-being, but only as a result of the more important elements — service of the public good, aggressive responsible individualism and culture . . . In the practical terms of everyday life, culture is not about agreement, but about questioning. In other words, culture is not about solidarity, but about discussion and disagreements.

We have seen that creativity and anxiety (provided that the latter is contained in some fashion) go hand in hand. As Stacey (1996b, pp. 181–2) says, we need to strive for levels of 'holding environments' within which we can pursue creative solutions:

> Part of the good enough holding environment is provided by an organization's members themselves; the holding is good enough if they trust and like each other to a reasonable extent . . . Another element is the large system of which an organization is a part — the industry and society of which it is a member. Thus, the manner in which others in a society treat an organization affects the level of anxiety the organization experiences and what it then finds it must do to contain it . . . When an industry and society provide a supportive emotional environment for an organization, its members are able to hold higher levels of anxiety and therefore may be more creative. However, punishing, insecure, or highly pressurized societies are likely to drive organizations to create

their own anxiety-containing structures at the expense of organizational creativity.

Could there be a more classic case of this problem than schools? Punishing strategies in the holding environment indeed! Such strategies, evident in many jurisdictions, actually *reduce* creativity and lead to dysfunctional forms of coping with stress. Ironically they produce the very opposite to what is intended. Instead of innovation, we get greater resistance. Stacey, in other words, presents a more sophisticated version of the outside-in analysis I discussed in chapter 4, namely that outside agencies can be most influential in school reform when they balance and integrate stimulus and accountability on the one hand (which raises anxiety) and local capacity-building and trust on the other hand (which enables locals to contain anxiety within reasonable bounds). Note the phrase 'balance and integrate'. This is not just a matter of introducing various elements of pressure and support. Strategies of pressure and support that are segmented from each other simply work at cross purposes. Pressure and support must be integrated and must flow within the interaction of internal and external forces. In effect, holding environments in the organization (chapter 3) or in relation to the environment (chapter 4) are places where anxiety is stimulated but plays itself out creatively within supportive relationships.

One can also see that the overall strategy required is not easy to obtain. Mintzberg, Ahlstrand and Lampel (1998) show that no management model is able to grasp the whole elephant. Their careful conclusion after reviewing ten different models is that 'strategic formation is a complex space' (Mintzberg *et al.*, 1998, p. 372). The problem is in the process itself, i.e. it is the nature of the beast.

> Strategy formation is judgmental designing, intuitive visioning, and emergent learning; it is about transformation as well as perpetuation; it must involve individual cognition and social interaction, cooperation as well as conflict; it has to include analyzing before and programming after as well as negotiating during; and all of this must be in response to what can be a demanding environment. Just try to leave any of this out and watch what happens! (Mintzberg *et al.*, 1998, p. 373)

It is challenges like this that led Clemmer (cited in Mintzberg) to conclude that 'change management is an oxymoron.' If we can't manage change in the sense of controlling it, what can we do?

The lessons in this book provide a framework for thinking, for design and for action. To say that postmodern society is incredibly complex does not mean that all planning is out the window. In bringing together the overarching messages of the preceding chapters, three main planning orientations should be emphasized: (a) the importance of understanding and using the forces of change, (b) the way in which planning must be based on the deeper insights we have discussed in previous chapters, and (c) the power of fostering and fusing intellectual, political and spiritual forces.

Understand and Use the Forces of Change to Your Advantage

The first and foremost step is to understand what makes social forces move forward in turbulent environments. It is much like whitewater rafting. If you try to overmanage it, you capsize. Rather than steering away from upcoming rocks, you move toward the danger, guiding the craft in relation to the forces coming at you. In previous chapters, we have seen that the deeper meaning of coping with change forces requires living between too much and too little structure in which people derive new directions as they encounter diversity inside and outside the organization.

As Stacey (1996b, p. 282) states, we need to 'reflect in public on what we are doing, using the science of complexity to inform that self-reflection [because] the speed of change is faster than ever before and the level of complexity we must all deal with is greater than ever before.' We have also seen that good outcomes are not as random as they may seem in such a system. There are orientations and conditions that we can work on that make it likely that positive patterns will frequently emerge. For Stacey (1996b, p. 179) they include 'the rate of information flow, the degree of diversity, the richness of connectivity, the level of contained anxiety, and the degree of power differentials' (the latter being the balance between directive forms of leadership and bottom-up initiative).

The first step, then, involves understanding the complex, interactive flow of change, establishing conditions that will turn this complexity to advantage, and then looking for, fostering, reinforcing and celebrating emerging outcomes that are valued, while discouraging those that are not.

Base Planning on Deeper Insights

Since effective planning operates in complex space, it must be based on deep insights. Techniques or tools are just that — they are only tools which should never be treated as ends in themselves. They are effective only when used in the service of a more powerful underlying conception. This difference between good and bad (or absent) conceptions is why we sometimes see a given technique or model or program succeed in one situation and fail in another. The Comer program (or Reading Recovery, Accelerated Schools, etc.) works in one case but goes nowhere in another. The model matters (i.e. it must be of good quality), but in the hands of someone without a strong underlying conception of change it will fail.

Thus you don't just build collaborative cultures as a model or as an end in itself; your actions must be informed and driven by ideas that the development of learning communities specifically generates greater learning (chapter 3). Designing relationships to the outside and vice versa must be founded on the realization that reciprocity — two-way influence — is the only way to go (chapter 4). And transferability must be conceived as not just product dissemination, but also as figuring out how to replicate the conditions that resulted in successful change in the first place (chapter 5). And so on.

In all cases, planning is not following a particular model but rather it is working on an underlying conception of change in which techniques and tools are resources in the service of bigger goals. There is a place for careful strategy formulation in complex change processes, but it has to do with the conceptions and design criteria that inform day-to-day actions. Schools as learning communities in their inside and outside relations will not happen by chance. They require assertive planning, the depth and likes of which we have rarely seen.

Foster and Fuse Intellectual, Political and Spiritual Forces

The third big step is to recognize that intellectual, political and spiritual forces must be developed and combined. Schools and school systems are traditionally weak on these dimensions, but when they do move in these directions, they get solid results, with promises of much more to come. Thus, the need is to foster and fuse intellectual, political and spiritual energies — to have these powerful forces feed on each other.

Let me recap why, especially in schools, we have to foster the development of intellectual, political and spiritual forces. We don't often think of teachers as being in the business of scientific breakthroughs. Yet that is exactly what the intellectual dimension needs to become. A flow of new and better knowledge and ideas is the lifeblood of continuous improvement. Yet school systems are not known for their capacity to seek and incorporate new ideas, and there is no strong external infrastructure that supports schools in this regard. We saw earlier that successful schools have started down the path of considering and using new ideas, but even the best have not yet gone very far. Now that these schools and school systems are getting results on basic learning outcomes, the next question becomes how they can truly go deeper helping students construct their own meaning, become problem-solvers, work in diverse groups and otherwise prepare themselves for a lifetime of proactive citizenship in a complex world. In light of recent developments in the science of pedagogy, there is a great deal of potential in brain research, cognitive science, group work, emotional intelligence, technology and the like. But so far, seeking the best knowledge for specific problems has not become habitual for schools. Knowledge-creation using the world of ideas about learning is therefore one of the three core fusion forces.

A second key dimension is mobilizing power to get things done. Schools have shied away from using politics for positive purposes. The field of politics has been largely in the hands of comparatively extreme forces on the left and the right resulting in even greater polarization. These power struggles occasionally result in victory for one side or the other, but never result in winning the war! Winning the war means reconciling differences which can never be done by extremes. So the political component involves establishing alliances among diverse parties inside and outside the school. You can't alter a complex system unless you mobilize a critical mass of different groups working together. Make no mistake about it, successful large-scale change does involve the use of power. But it is power used in the service of a compelling moral purpose, which is the third core element.

Moral purpose or the spiritual dimension of education reform involves elevating the debate and commitment to making a difference in the lives of all students. I believe that this goal has been latent in the hearts of many educators and citizens and is on the ascendancy. Why did Goleman's (1995) book on *Emotional Intelligence* become an instant million-dollar seller? Why do we see more and more books with the words soul, spirit, meaning in the title? The research Goleman presented has been accumulating for some years. The reason the book flew off the shelves was *timing*; it hit a concealed rich vein of discontent and hope. The majority of people, I think, are growing weary of conflict in society, the widening gap of the haves and the have nots, the cold hand of technology and other forms of impersonality and degradation of humanity. Instead, people have a deepening interior need to find and give meaning to life. There are few professions other than teaching where gaining personal meaning through improving the lives of others for years and even generations to come is so palpable and profound. But concern for a better life for oneself and others is also a wider trend in society which led the pollster, Angus Reid (1996, p. 218), to predict that 'over the next few decades, an emphasis on emotional growth will overtake the post-war preoccupation with material well-being.' All of this augurs well, not only for the moral purpose of teaching, but also for the likelihood that spiritual forces will find political and intellectual allies.

It is also clear why we need the power of fusion, i.e. the three sets of forces interacting and combining for maximum effect. Ideas without moral purpose are a dime a dozen. Moral purpose without ideas means being all dressed up with nowhere to go. Power without ideas or moral purpose is deadly. Moral purpose and ideas without power means the train never leaves the station. The interactive systems I described in chapters 3 to 5 — the deep meaning of collaboration to obtain substantial results — are precisely systems that gain their tremendous energy through the fusion of intellectual, political and spiritual purposes. At their best, they do this at the individual, organizational and system levels in concert:

> One theme in all types of fusion [interaction] is that organizational and personal fusion reinforce each other. Individuals discover their own wholeness in a fusion relationship with others. And organizational fusion needs the leadership and enthusiasm of participants to transform the larger system. Fusion is accomplished through conversation across traditional boundaries that meets people's yearnings to be part of something larger than themselves, to face reality and new challenges, to create a shared future together, and to take action that serves others and the organization. Fusion leaders understand how to orchestrate fusion to achieve bursts of motivation and change. (Daft and Lengel, 1998, p. 235)

Full and complete fusion as applied to social systems is a metaphor, but it is a powerful and accurate one. We have seen throughout this book that fusion involves joining and connecting differences, creating coherence and coming together under stressful and uncertain conditions. And when it occurs *it produces five times the energy* — the kind of energy that is essential for self-organizing breakthroughs in complex systems, the kind of energy that can never be orchestrated through models that attempt to plan and manage change.

I have argued that leaders at all levels from the classroom to the state house need to conceptualize and continue to construct ever more sophisticated practical theories of action. These theories of action will enable them: to understand the critical importance of incorporating all three forces — the intellectual, the political, and the spiritual — in their thinking and action; to constantly work at connections across these forces and across people; and to build the local and external designs and infrastructures required for interaction and fusion of energy.

Too often in education even the most exciting possibilities have fallen flat, leading to greater demoralization and cynicism. Even great ideas need hard work to be realized. Cohen (1998, p. 445) puts it forcefully:

> But inspiring visions and hope also can keep reformers from building the intellectual and social infrastructure that is needed for abiding reform: devising strategy and tactics, making plans and building organization, systematically investigating the process and progress of reform and its impact, and thus creating opportunities to learn from experience. Reformers need 'unrealistic' hope as much as teachers do, but such vision alone can enable them to ignore the difficult work in which hope would be given legs and direction, in which hope could be informed by systematic learning and thus be given means to sustain itself and improve through the inevitable frustrations and failure . . . One distinguishing feature of more exemplary teachers is that they not only hope but also devise the strategies, make or adapt the curriculum, consider classroom tactics, learn from students' work and their own, and in other ways create the intellectual and social infrastructure that enables their students to capitalize both on the visions that inspire their practice and on the hope that sustains it and that enables them to learn from their work.

The purpose of educational reform in other words is to create systems that will enable us to go to scale in giving hope legs. It should also be abundantly clear why we have argued that educators must take the debate to the public. Fusion depends on 'capturing the public imagination' and the only way to do that is to get out there and engage communities in the debate about ideas, power and purpose. Policymakers at the same time must ensure that they are working to raise the status of teachers. As they establish greater expectations and standards, policymakers must know that none of this can be accomplished without supporting local forces to mobilize the will and skill of teachers. Successful external initiatives end up reducing the frustration of and unleashing the energies of hitherto frustrated and demoralized teachers. The interaction between external and internal forces in these instances provides the mechanism for taking bold steps toward the future.

The Unfinished Business on the Evolutionary Chain

Reflecting on the evolution of humankind at the end of the twentieth century, one can't help but think that we are on the brink of a new age. The future could go in one of two opposite directions. It could march down the path of self-interest, with greater gaps between the haves and the have nots and a continuing deterioration of democracy and the common good. Or the negative forces of postmodernity could play themselves out. We could, in evolutionary terms, not so much reclaim higher ground but move to it! To accomplish the latter will take the exquisite appreciation and actions of self-aware educators who realize this could be a watershed in our evolution as human beings. Humans among all species possess something special — the potential to reach more advanced forms of evolution or to squander the opportunity. The public school system will turn out to be one major test ground for advancement or regression on the evolutionary chain of human development.

All this sounds pretty lofty when you are facing your worst class on a Friday afternoon. But when you team up with other teachers and parents to teach a group of 7-year-olds to read and write for the first time, or you change the future of a 16-year-old otherwise destined to a life of misery, you don't have to be aware of human evolution to contribute to it. We have a long way to go on the evolutionary chain, but teachers with moral purpose will always be key players in any progress we make.

Those engaged in educational reform are those engaged in societal development; those engaged in societal development are those engaged in the evolution of virtue. It is time to return to large-scale reform with even more ambitious goals than we had in the 1960s, armed with the sophisticated knowledge that we can turn complexity's own hidden power to our advantage. Interaction, quality information and moral purpose represent powerful forces for the public good. It is time to infuse meaning into the millennium while we seize complexity. It is time, in other words, to harness the forces of fusion. 'Change forces' remains a double entendre of exciting proportions.

References

BERTELSMANN, C. (1996) *Innovative School Systems in an International Comparison*, Gütersloh, Germany, Bertelsmann Foundation Publishers.

BROWN, S. and EISENHARDT, K. (1998) *Competing on the Edge*, Boston, MA, Harvard Business School Press.

BRYK, A., SEBRING, P., KERBOW, D., ROLLOW, S. and EASTON, J. (1998a) *Charting Chicago School Reform*, Boulder, CO, Westview Press.

BRYK, A., THUM, Y., EASTON, J. and LUPPESCU, S. (1998b) *Academic Productivity of Chicago Elementary Schools*, Chicago, University of Chicago Consortium on School Research.

COBURN, C. and MEYER, E. (1998) 'Shaping context to support and sustain reform', paper presented at the American Education Research Association.

COHEN, D. (1998) 'Dewey's problem', *The Elementary School Journal*, 98, 5, pp. 427–46.

COLEMAN, J. (1990) *Foundations of Social Theory*, Cambridge, MA, Harvard University Press.

COLEMAN, P. (1998) *Parent, Student and Teacher Collaboration: The Power of Three*, Thousand Oaks, CA, Corwin Press.

DAFT, R. and LENGEL, R. (1998) *Fusion Leadership*, San Francisco, Berrett-Koehler.

DAMASIO, A. (1994) *Descartes' Error*, New York, Grosset Putnam.

DARLING-HAMMOND, L. (1997) *National Commission on Teaching and America's Future: Final Progress Report*, New York, Teachers College, Columbia University.

DE GUES, A. (1997) *The Living Company*, Cambridge, MA, Harvard Business School Press.

DEPARTMENT FOR EDUCATION AND EMPLOYMENT (1997) *The Implementation of the National Literacy Strategy*, London, DfEE.

EARL, L. and LEE, L. (1998) *School Improvement: What Have We Learned From the Manitoba Experience*, Toronto, Walter and Duncan Gordon Foundation.

References

ELMORE, R. (1995) 'Getting to scale with good educational practice', *Harvard Educational Review*, **66**, 1, pp. 1–26.

ELMORE, R. and BURNEY, D. (1998) *School Variation and Systemic Instructional Component in Community School District #2, New York City*, University of Pennsylvania, Consortium for Policy Research in Education.

EPSTEIN, J., COATES, L., SALINAS, K., SANDERS, M. and SIMON, B. (1997) *School, Family and Community Partnership: Your Handbook for Action*, Thousand Oaks, CA, Corwin Press.

FULLAN, M. (1993) *Change Forces: Probing the Depths of Educational Reform*, London, Falmer Press.

FULLAN, M. (1997) *What's Worth Fighting For in the Principalship?*, 2nd edn, Toronto, Ontario Public School Teachers' Federation; New York, Teachers College Press; Buckingham, Open University Press.

FULLAN, M. (1998) 'Leadership for change in faculties of education', in D. THIESSEN and K. HOWEY (eds), *Agents Provocateur: Reform Minded Leaders for Schools of Education*, Washington, DC, American Association of College for Teacher Education, pp. 29–48.

FULLAN, M. and HARGREAVES, A. (1992) *What's Worth Fighting For? Working Together for Your School*, Toronto, Ontario Public School Teachers' Federation; New York, Teachers College Press; Buckingham, Open University Press.

FULLAN, M. and WATSON, N. (1998) *Building Infrastructures for Professional Development*, New York, The Rockefeller Foundation.

GALBRAITH, J. (1996) *The Good Society*, Boston, Houghton, Mifflin.

GOERNER, S. (1998) 'Web world and the turning of times', unpublished manuscript.

GOLEMAN, D. (1995) *Emotional Intelligence*, New York, Bantam Books.

GOLEMAN, D. (1998) *Working with Emotional Intelligence*, New York, Bantam Books.

THE GORDON FOUNDATION (1998) *Manitoba School Improvement Program*, The Walter and Duncan Gordon Foundation, Toronto, Author.

GROVE, A. (1996) *Only the Paranoid Survive*, New York, Doubleday.

HARGREAVES, A. and FULLAN, M. (1998) *What's Worth Fighting for Out There?* Toronto, Elementary School Teachers' Federation; New York, Teachers' College Press; Buckingham, Open University Press.

HATCH, J. (1998) 'The differences in theory that matter in the practice of school improvement', *American Educational Research Journal*, **35**, 1, pp. 3–81.

HEALEY, F. and DE STEFANO, J. (1997) *Education Reform Support: A Framework for Scaling up School Reform*, Washington, DC, Abel 2 Clearinghouse for Basic Education.

HEIFETZ, R. (1994) *Leadership without Easy Answers*, Cambridge, MA, Harvard University Press.

HILL, P. and CELIO, M. (1998) 'Fixing urban schools', unpublished report, The Brookings Institution Press.

LEONARD, D. (1995) *Wellsprings of Knowledge*, Boston, MA, Harvard Business School Press.

LEWIS, C., BATTISTICH, V., SCHAPS, E., SOLOMON, D. and WATSON, M. (1998) *School Improvement for Academic Development and Resilience: Findings from the Child Development Project*, Oakland, CA, Development Studies Center.

LOUIS, K. and KRUSE, S. (eds) (1995) *Professionalism and Community*, Thousand Oaks, CA, Corwin Press.

MAURER, R. (1996) *Beyond the Wall of Resistance*, Austin, TX, Bard Books.

MICKLETHWAIT, J. and WOOLDRIDGE, A. (1996) *The Witch Doctors: Making Sense of Management Gurus*, New York, Times Books, Random House.

MINTZBERG, H. (1994) *The Rise and Fall of Strategic Planning*, New York, Free Press.

MINTZBERG, H., AHLSTRAND, B. and LAMPEL, J. (1998) *Strategy Safari: A Guided Tour through the Wilds of Strategic Management*, New York, Free Press.

NATIONAL COMMISSION ON TEACHING AND AMERICA'S FUTURE (1996) *What Matters Most: Teaching for America's Future*, Washington, DC, NCFTA.

NEWMANN, F. and WEHLAGE, G. (1995) *Successful School Restructuring*, Madison, WI, Center on Organization and Restructuring of Schools.

NONAKA, I. and TAKEUCHI, H. (1995) *The Knowledge-Creating Company*, Oxford, Oxford University Press.

OAKES, J., WELNER, K., YONEZAWN, S. and ALLEN, R. (1998) 'Norms and politics of equity-minded change', in A. HARGREAVES, A. LIEBERMAN, M. FULLAN and D. HOPKINS (eds), *International Handbook of Educational Change*, Dondrecht: Kluwer Academic Publishers, pp. 952–73.

OATLEY, K. and JENKINS, J. (1996) *Understanding Emotions*, Cambridge, MA, Blackwell.

ORBIT (1998) 'From reform to renewal', Special issue, 29, 1, Toronto, Ontario Institute for Studies in Education, University of Toronto.

PASCALE, A. (1990) *Managing on the Edge*, New York, Simon & Schuster.

REID, A. (1996) *Shakedown: How the Economy Is Changing Our Lives*, Toronto, Doubleday.

RIDLEY, M. (1996) *The Origins of Virtue*, London, Penguin Books.

SAUL, J. (1995) *The Unconscious Civilization*, Toronto, Anansi Press.

References

SAUL, J. (1997) *Reflections of a Siamese Twin*, London, Penguin Books.

SCHORR, L. (1997) *Common Purpose: Strengthening Families and Neighborhoods to Rebuild America*, New York, Doubleday, Anchor Books.

SEBRING, P. and BRYK, A. (1998) *School Leadership and the Bottom Line in Chicago*, Chicago, University of Chicago, Consortium on School Research.

SENGE, P. (1990) *The Fifth Discipline*, New York, Doubleday.

SKYNNER, R. and CLEESE, J. (1993) *Life and How to Survive It*, London, Methuen.

SLEE, R., WEINER, G. and TOMLINSON, S. (1998) *School Effectiveness for Whom?*, London, Falmer Press.

SOBER, E. and WILSON, D. (1998) *Unto Others: The Evolution and Psychology of Unselfish Behavior*, Cambridge, MA, Harvard University Press.

STACEY, R. (1996a) *Strategic Management and Organizational Dynamics*, 2nd edn, London, Pitman.

STACEY, R. (1996b) *Complexity and Creativity in Organizations*, San Francisco, Berrett-Koehler.

STOKES, L., SATO, N., McLAUGHLIN, M. and TALBERT, J. (1997) *Theory-based Reform and Problems of Change Contexts that Matter for Teachers' Learning and Community*, Stanford, CA, Final Report to the Mellon Foundation.

STORR, A. (1997) *Feet of Clay: A Study of Gurus*, London: Harper Collins.

VIDEO JOURNAL OF EDUCATION (1998) *What's Worth Fighting For in Education?*, Salt Lake City, UT, VJE (two-hour video based on *What's Worth Fighting For?* trilogy).

WALLACE, M. and POCKLINGTON, K. (1998) 'Slipping through the cracks: Policy interaction and implementation of school reorganization initiatives', paper presented at the American Educational Research Association.

WILKINSON, R. (1996) *Unhealthy Societies*, London, Routledge.

Index

accountability 52–3, 56–60, 69
Ahlstrand, B. 78
anxiety 24–7, 37–8, 61, 77–8

Bertelsmann 53, 69
Brown, S. 5–6, 13–14, 23–4, 37, 40,
    47–8, 51, 66
Bryk, A. 19, 27, 34–6, 38–40, 46–8,
    51–3, 56–7, 59, 64, 69, 73
Burney, D. 19, 48–50, 69

capacity building 52–3, 56–7, 65–6,
    68–70, 74–5
Celio, M. 71–3
change lessons 17–30
change theories 20–2, 28–30, 71–5,
    77–84
chaos theory *see* complexity theory
Chicago reform 34–6, 46, 51–3, 69
Cleese, J. 26
Coburn, C. 65
Cohen, D. 10, 83
coherence 27–8, 39–40, 54–5, 70
Coleman, J. 11
Coleman, P. 61
collaborative cultures 26–7, 59–62,
    71–4
    inside collaboration 31–41
    inside-out collaboration 43–8
    outside-in collaboration 48–59
community 45–6, 52–3, 61
complexity theory 3–6, 10–12,
    23–4, 51–2, 59–60, 67–8,
    79–80
conflict *see* diversity
consensus *see* diversity

Daft, R. 77, 82
Damasio, A. 37–8
Darling-Hammond, L. 56
De Gues, A. 7, 13, 22, 43
De Stefano, J. 56, 64, 66, 70
Department for Education and
    Employment 58
Dewey, John 66
    referred to by Cohen 10
    referred to by Elmore 66
District #2, New York City 48–51, 69
diversity 2–3, 22–6, 36–7, 77
Durham School District 53, 69

Earl, L. 33, 47, 53
Easton, J. 52
Eisenhardt, D. 5–6, 13–14, 23–4, 37,
    40, 47–8, 51, 66
Elmore, R. 19, 23, 48–50, 66–7, 69,
    70
emotional intelligence *see* anxiety
Epstein, J. 61
equity *see* diversity
evolutionary theory 6–12, 84

Galbraith, J. 11
Goerner, S. 10
Goleman, D. 25, 40, 81
The Gordon Foundation 33–4, 53
Grove, A. 40

Hargreaves, A. 11, 23, 31, 45, 58, 61
Hatch, J. 21
Healey, F. 56, 64, 66, 70
Heifetz, R. 23, 25–6
Hill, P. 71–3

Change Forces

Probing the Depths of Educational Reform
Michael Fullan, OISE, University of Toronto, Canada

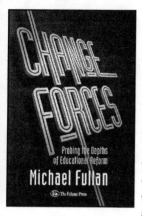

"This book is excellent. It says all the things I want teachers to hear and act upon about managing their own learning, about balancing life and work, and about how schools need to invest in teacher learning and look to how they become learning organisations. It does provide clarity and insights for understanding and coping with educational reform, as it says on the cover, and it does explain the new 'mind set' needed for 'contending with the real complexities of dynamic and continuous change'." *Management Learning, 1995*

"Written in a style that can almost be called exciting if not mind blowing, the author debunks many of the current myths and ideas ... An absolute must for educationalists, irrespective of their place in the system." *Institute of Health Education, 1995*

1 85000 825 6	HB	£36.00
1 85000 826 4	PB	£13.95
172pp	1993	

Change Forces: The Sequel

Michael Fullan, OISE, University of Toronto, Canada

Fullan's first book on this subject was an instant and best-selling success. Now, in *Change Forces: The Sequel* he extends and expands the use of chaos theory, as a lens through which to view and comprehend change, and the forces which govern it. Educators have already widely embraced this approach, and taken on board the idea that change is not so straightforward as we might hope. As Fullan worked on his ideas, relating them to school systems, higher education and research, the field of change forces also developed significantly. This volume will cover the new aspects of this 'science of complexity' and help educators obtain insights for delving deeper into moral purpose, and expanding into fresh dimensions of changing forces in the environment.

0 7507 0756 9	HB	£42.00
0 7507 0755 0	PB	£13.95
120pp		